72 HOURS
UNSCRIPTED

How to Navigate the Ultimate 3-Day Bravoleb Weekend

LISA HENDRICKSON

INTRODUCTION

Welcome, Bravoholics! If you've ever dreamed of attending BravoCon, the ultimate gathering of Bravo TV stars, superfans, and nonstop drama, then this book is for you. As a passionate BravoCon expert and the CEO/Founder of the amazing BravoCon Facebook community for BravoCon fans, I've seen firsthand how BravoCon comes to life in Las Vegas, transforming from online to reality. And trust me, there is drama at BravoCon, but most of it is the best unscripted drama you will ever see!

One of the questions most asked in the BravoCon Facebook Group is, well...everything about BravoCon! After 2023, I decided I needed to write an book to help guide everyone and answer all the questions you will have when you start your preparation for the event.

This book will help you navigate your way to enjoying a thrilling 72-hour journey of BravoCon. I cover everything from preparing for your trip to buying tickets, selling tickets, what to expect, tips for solos, helping with your budget, all the activations and experiences you can attend, and finally, well... just everything! But I leave out enough for you to have the time of your life! I promise nothing you read will ruin a thing for you but only make you better prepared. BravoCon is a lot and extra, and we all love extras!

A few notes before you start with Chapter One: I go in depth in each chapter with stories and my own experiences. Honestly, I loved writing this book so much and when I was done, I missed writing it. I shared so many tips and tricks, stories and memories, it could be considered my BravoCon diary.

Before you start, you might also want to go to my Patreon page https://www.patreon.com/UnofficialGuidetoBravoCon and sign up as a free member. Free members will get updates (my version of newsletters). I do offer a tier you can subscribe to; the tiers have some other "paid access" options. You can also follow me on my social media accounts, which I have listed at the end of the book. I'll be sharing videos, more tips, and other fun stories!

I look forward to seeing you all at BravoCon! Enjoy!

TABLE OF CONTENTS

CHAPTER 1

THE BRAVOCON FACEBOOK GROUP

The Beginning of the BravoCon Facebook Group

I started the Facebook BravoCon group in May of 2019. I was in a few other Bravo TV-related Facebook groups, and when BravoCon was announced, I knew I had to go. A few of us chatted about a meetup, so I went to Facebook and made a group. We didn't know much to post about, and eventually, the group seemed dead. I sat in that group alone for a while, but little did I know that a few Bravo fans found the group and joined but stayed silent. In the past couple of years, some OG's (slang for original) of the group have told me they joined two weeks after I created the group, so they got the OG title in the BravoCon FB group. We are now close to celebrating our 5th anniversary!

I'm going to guess it was around July 2019 that more people started joining because of ticket sales marketing. I was not in shock, but really in shock. I was the only group on Facebook with the word "BravoCon," and by the end of July, there were a few hundred people in the group. The marketing for BravoCon back then was a bit tough to follow; it was their first year, and the messaging, as you can imagine for a first-year convention, was "figure it out as you go," a fair assumption. As it was NBC's first BravoCon, we all had to learn together. A little memory I have is that you had to email a Gmail address for information about tickets. It's kind of cute if you think about it. A huge TV network is out doing their first convention with no experience, winging it and using Gmail, wild! It's only been 5 years, but it shows how far this experience has grown and how long a way it's come.

As the group started to grow, I was managing it alone and didn't know what to do or how to handle it. All I know is that people were posting information and asking each other questions, and there I was, trying to make sense of it all. I also don't use Instagram much and was out of the loop on so many people talking about it. I did what a good momager does and just ran the command center.

I believe tickets were going on sale in August of that year, and that's when the group had over 500 people. It was crazy with everyone trying to figure out tickets as information was released. I also had to make a tough decision. I learned that the event had many different locations, and I had just reinjured my arthritic leg. Deciding to go would be agonizing. I was a bit scared about being alone in NYC, but I had all these online friends now, so I wasn't going to be completely alone. However, my physical issues were my own problem, so I decided not to go, and it broke my heart. Getting around quickly would have been too much and most likely frustrating.

Having made that decision, I turned my attention to the group, which was already out of control, and put out a post asking for help to moderate. I wanted someone who was going to the event, so they could post pictures and do the street team help I might need. I had a few volunteers, and then Suzy messaged me.

Suzy McGonigle, my 5 years+ Bravo Bestie (seriously, if you don't have one, please find one in the group—there is nothing more satisfying than texting your bestie during the workday with Bravo drama!), said she would help me. Suzy and I became thick as thieves that summer and managed the group in a manner that I didn't know we would need. We had so much to do! We tried to figure out the schedules, events, and everything Bravo had going on. It was like a matrix for the first year. Between us not knowing what was going on, we did our best and, yep, faked it until we made it!

Finally, by the time the event came, everyone in the group was exhausted from figuring out schedules, events, the 3 locations, all the activities to do, BravoPalooza, WWHL, and everything in between. I will never forget that Thursday before the event started when the pictures and videos started popping up in the group. It was never-ending. I was running the group from my house while Suzy was on location in Manhattan trying to keep up and admin the group. It was truly the most fun we both ever had. For the next three days, this Facebook group had over 110,000 posts, comments, and views. I think by the end of the event, there were 2000 people in the group.

We did have a meetup! Suzy organized the first real meetup, which had about 30 attendees. The group was created to have a meetup with the 20 or so gals, so I already achieved a goal. I just wasn't there!

After the weekend, when everyone went home, even more pictures and videos were posted that week, and we got some attention. Suzy and I started seeing some media folks join the group and employees at NBC/Bravo TV. We were both shocked. Facebook groups are not like IG; they are small private communities, and to get new members from our beloved event join felt awesome!

We closed the 2019 BravoCon season on such a high, and then we were all hit with the news in March 2020. 2020 and 2021 were tough years. I don't want to recap the emotional feelings I experienced, but both BravoCon's were announced and canceled. 2021 was the worst, as we had already planned so much for it. Boo.

Finally, in April of 2022, we got the email from Bravo! We're on, and you're involved; let's get this going on! At this point, life was kind of back to normal, so we decided to go all in. Bravo gave us some information to share with the group. This was amazing, not only for the members but for me and Suzy. We literally felt starstruck!

Then, things took a different turn in the group very quickly. We went from around 2000 or so members to approximately

4000 members during the next few months. While that doesn't seem like a lot in comparison to an Instagram account, it was a lot for us. Suzy and I watched the little mighty group grow and slow down during the few years of Covid, so hitting 4000 members was a huge milestone.

During the summer of 2022, the group started to really feel like a community of fans. We all helped each other navigate BravoCon 2022. There was a better structure that we could all figure out. Lindsey Clark created the best schedule and shared it on Google Docs, a feat that would forever be blessed for us. It is a spreadsheet with colors and tabs of all the events, locations and times. Truly, the easiest way to navigate your schedule in one place.

Many members started to make friends in the group. Meetups were created and, yep, hotels were secured by myself. I talked to many hotels about a group rate, and I got it. I secured a large contract with two hotels and got everyone a great group rate so we could all be together. One hotel, the Marriott Courtyard, was close to Javits and had a bar, and we could hold our meetup—my original goal of creating the group in 2019!

By the time BravoCon 2022 started, the group had 7000 members. Suzy and I were so excited; everything was planned, and we were ready to roll! I was flying into JFK, got my own car and literally felt like a Bravoleb. Due to my injury and size (bigger girl here), I just wanted to make sure I was comfortable. I got to the hotel early, and all hell broke loose. I was talking to Facebook BravoCon members all day long, it seemed. You can just spot one of us—we are all happy and smiling!

The whole weekend was like a dream; the hotel was close for a quick Uber to Javits for me, we figured out the Javits center on day one, and we were off in the Bravoverse. Suzy and I did hang out a lot that weekend, but we also gave each other time to explore and find new fun things to share. We texted each other, "OMG, come to the Bravo Bazaar now!" and we would rush to meet, hang out, have fun, and then split up. The best part of BravoCon is that you can go alone or meet others and have the time of your life. I will talk about going solo in chapter 16.

Again, we closed another BravoCon season, and it took many weeks to recover. So many members posted about missing how they felt that weekend; they wanted to experience it again, and I think our group formed an awesome bond. I was a proud mama.

At the close of the 2022 event, the group had 10,000 members and while we waited for the 2023 announcement, you know what happened in Feb/March of 2023? Scandoval hit like wildfire, and our group blew up again! Suzy and I were not prepared for this surge, and we also had to prepare for BravoCon 2023. In April of 2023, Bravo announced that 2023 was going to be in Vegas, and we were on! With Scandoval and BravoCon, the group had posted all day long, buzzing with new members. It's like a small city, practically. We had 7 months to plan for a 3-day weekend. I still giggle when I say that, but BravoCon is literally our own Super Bowl. We had a lot of planning to do. Vegas was going to be way bigger and required a lot more planning, and I was ready!

That's the history, my B's! Somehow, in the past few years, I was crowned the title of "Queen of BravoCon" by the lovely members, and I wear the crown proudly. I call you all "My B's," as it's endearing for me to say. I feel it, and it shows my love for the community. I will use it often in this book.

So, let's roll! I'm beyond thrilled you have plans to go to BravoCon. It's certainly an event of a lifetime if you haven't gone yet. My book will give you step-by-step guidance on how to do practically everything you need to know about BravoCon.

CHAPTER 2

TIMELINES AND INDEX

Now that my introduction about myself is done, I will start getting into the good stuff. If you have been a member of the BravoCon Facebook Group for a while now, this part might be a recap. If you haven't gone to BravoCon and are new to the group, this will be very helpful.

Many members in our group have said, "This is our Super Bowl," and it is equivalent, but the Super Bowl is not an intense 5-day jam-packed weekend with 1000 things to do. BravoCon is literally an interactive event from the time you start preparing to attend. You pack your glam and swag, arrive in Vegas, enjoy the Thursday night meetup, get into 3 full days and nights of BravoCon, and then fly home completely exhausted with two little legs that can barely walk. You will not have time to relax; you will not have time to breathe; you will not watch TV; you will not be scrolling any other social media, you will not do anything but be 100% absorbed with Bravo for the entire time.

The BravoCon Facebook group starts lighting up many days before we all take off to fly to Vegas. Starting on Thursday and if you want to keep up in the group, you better scroll fast because there are so many posts, it's hard to keep up. If you are not going, you can definitely feel like you are there with everything that is posted. The group is so full of pictures of people arriving at the airport, Bravoleb sightings, who is doing what—it's wild. After BravoCon, the group is so full of happiness for weeks. Everyone shares their pictures, tells stories, and reminisces about the best time of their life. You will not find another community on the internet like ours, with the loyalty and fandom of BravoCon.

This is why my B's, you all need to prepare, save up money, and know everything so you are ready. While it took many of us a while in 2022 to figure everything out, there is a method to the BravoCon madness, and you'll have all the information you need so no need to worry! And if there is a change, I'll be sure to update you in real time through my Patreon site.

If you have never been to BravoCon before, each year, it does seem that something about the event (activations, Bravolebs attending, etc.) does change, but the agenda of the announcements from Bravo and the timeline stays pretty much the same. Right now, we are a long way off, but as I always say, things can change quickly. Example: We are used to tickets being on sale in July, but with a one-plus year notice of the event, tickets might go on sale this fall, next spring, or in July. My mind is spinning with what ifs, my B's!

One thing the Facebook group did together was figure out the timelines for how Bravo sends out the announcements. That's why the OG's of 2019 bonded so well—they were the first and they are also some of the most helpful in the group. Bravo releases information in order and usually starts with the big announcement, then moves on to ticket sales day, add-on sales for BravoPalooza, WWHL, then schedules, photo ops, etc.

In the spring of 2022, and after BravoCon was announced, we had the game plan in our heads of how Bravo would manage the information, and we were on track. 2023 followed suit, and while both were the same, more or less, some changes came up as expected. One thing I noticed for the 2022 event is that everything was much more organized from Bravo TV in terms of their releases. Like any major convention, there are changes and finding those changes online is sometimes can be challenging as there are so many sources! Bravo TV has text messages, their IG page, the Bravo Broadcast, email newsletters, etc. At this moment, I don't know of one central information site outside of their website (not available yet) to get all the information. *And I mean all the information.* Some things we need to know are not official news from BravoCon, so we had to figure it out ourselves. For example, Formula One in Vegas was news we all learned about from other sources. It was good information to have as we had to work around the construction. Many of us followed a Vegas IG account to hear about all things Vegas. This is information, by the way, that I will be sharing on my Patreon site, as it will be news coming out after the book is completely published.

I'm hoping this book is that source for everything! You know how all the big Bravo accounts on Instagram get information and then they all share the same content? That's exactly what I hope my book and Patreon page are for everyone—one source for all the information, not just what Bravo releases officially. My goal is for the Patreon site to have the most up-to-date information as I get it from Bravo TV and our Facebook Group. I'll also be reading the group like a hawk, so I will publish anything the members of the Facebook Group post about, such as a Bravoleb or someone not coming, recently fired (oops!), etc—the kind of details that Bravo TV does not announce on the BravoCon website. I'm crossing my fingers that I can keep up.

No need to worry about anything now. We have many months to go. But I will end with a tip: *Start saving up weekly if you want to have a big Vegas experience.* On the BravoCon Facebook Group, I often read about members who wanted to do expensive things and didn't realize how much money it was going to be. BravoCon, for the most part, is a vacation/amazing experience of a lifetime and if you can save up now bit by bit, your budget will be bigger when purchasing time comes. BravoCon can be done on a budget, or do it all without a budget. Either way, chapter 16 has more information about the budget. Many members made it happen on a budget and had a blast. You can, too!

CHAPTER 3

BRAVOCON ANNOUNCEMENT SCHEDULE

A ny BravoCon fan will tell you how much pressure they feel when announcements come from Bravo. You have to be ready for these announcements, have your computer/phone and any extra devices ready to go at the ticket sale time, or register for one of the scheduled events. It feels like a competition to see who can get the tickets first. But that's the energy BravoCon brings—excitement, a racing heart, and hopefully, good anxiousness.

Bravo has, in the past, announced everything about the event in order of how they want you to purchase tickets for everything. There is also an order of importance. Not everything requires a purchase; some of their announcements are just big information drops, and those are trickled in much closer to the event. These are important for you to follow along if you're really investing your time into having the time of your life.

Pro Tip: *Follow our BravoCon Facebook Group Featured Discussions. We keep everything pinned from last year so you can read up! https://www.Facebook.com/groups/BravoCon/ announcements*

#1 BravoCon Announcement

Already done! We can wipe that off the list, at the Forum in Vegas.

#2 Ticket sales announcement

I'm going to spill a little tea about me and Suzy here. Since we have been Bravo Besties for 5 years almost, we know when things are going to be happening and have our own texts rolling. Trust me when I say this: every single year, we text, "Tickets will be on sale in the next couple of weeks," and then each day, "Think it will be on Friday? It's how it was last year," and I giggle as we get excited but never know when we will get that email from Bravo. Then BOOM, one day, when we least expect it, we get the email from our contact about the ticket sales and information. At least, this is how it has been for 2022 and 2023 (hoping the same for other upcoming events). As Bravo enjoys our little growing BravoCon Facebook Group, the email they send Suzy and me are about "pre-sale" tickets that they allow us to post about before the public gets the announcement. We are not the only group to get these pre-sale tickets. The Bravo Insiders email list and a few other special socials announce this, so it's very important you are ready! Suzy and I will make a post about the pre-sale the day before.

Historically, based on the past BravoCon events, it's a 3-month wait until tickets go on sale from the day of the event announcement. For the next event, I'm going to make a huge projection that tickets will be on sale way before next July. My projection is next spring of next year. I know people will be making their own projections, and other accounts on IG and socials will be posting things they have heard and this and that. I am going to state, for the record, these are my own thoughts, not from anything I have heard. The reason I am guessing tickets will go on sale way earlier is that the BravoCon organizers have more time to create a bigger, bolder, more bravo experience than ever before. They know more from 2023 and give us more, and you know we have room for more! They can do more with the information as they have experience with hosting an event at the same venue.

#3 BravoPalooza Tickets (paid ticket purchase option)

These usually go on sale in mid-August. Considering my guess of ticket sale dates, you should expect a month or so after ticket sales, Bravopalooza should follow suit in sales. Chapter 13 is all about these tickets coming up, so don't fret. I'll tell all the tea if you're new.

#4 BravoCon Live Tickets WWHL/Bravos (paid ticket purchase option)

You can expect these tickets to go on sale in September for the big evening events on Friday/Saturday and Sunday nights. I will cover more about this in Chapter 12, but these should go on sale shortly after the Bravopalooza tickets.

#5 Bravolebs Attending List Published

Bravo will announce all the Bravolebs they invited to attend, and this list can change a bit, but for the most part, it's on the spot. Unless someone gets fired, these Bravolebs attend. And if you have favorites, you'll want your charts ready of who you want to meet, create your own schedule, and how you can manage your crazy BravoCon events for each day!

#6 BravoCon Facebook Group Starts Offering M2M Ticket Sales (member to member)

This year, the game will be changed 100%, my B's. Last year was a complete frenzy and I guarantee you we will not be doing it the same way. I saw, in real time, the scammers following everything I did to prevent them; it was like a BravoCon ticket circus. I was finding scammers, blocking them, and then finding them in other fake BravoCon Groups selling fake tickets. I even tried having people make videos, and the scammers copied those people's profiles and used the videos. I was going crazy keeping up! That's why I created the Patreon account. As you know, I worked my tail off helping so many people get tickets and not get scammed. I felt so bad for people but with this Patreon, I can do it better with paying subscribers and people subscribed to my newsletter list. If you are reading this, you're already on my "preferred waitlist" if you register for an account.

How I see this working: When someone wants to sell a ticket and post it in the Facebook Group, they will need to subscribe to my Patreon first (newsletter or paid), and then I will personally help with the ticket sale between members. Sellers will feel better if they are selling to someone who has a subscription, whose email I have verified, done a Facetime/Zoom with etc. Trust me, even people selling got nervous too. They were afraid of a chargeback from the buyer. I'm hoping that my few extra steps help everyone with buying and selling a bit safer.

Paid subscribers and newsletter subscribers will have access to a community chat to discuss topics about BravoCon. I know that everyone is not on Facebook so having an outside community managed by someone (me!) will be great for those only using TikTok, Instagram/Threads.

#7 Schedules

And this is the #1 awaited announcement after ticket sales. Everyone wants to see the schedule of events for the 3-day event. It's a huge deal! The schedule is typically announced in Sept or 1+ months before BravoCon. If I'm on track with the early ticket sales, then again, I can't project when the schedules will be released, but it's def two months after tickets are out.

#8 BravoCon Mobile App Release

If you went in 2022 or 2023 and kept the app on your phone, then slowly, around 1 month before the event, give or take a week or so, the app will refresh, and you'll see the most awesome almost everything about BravoCon on the app. You can select all the events you want to attend and create your own schedule with the app! Some of us create paper charts, and some create spreadsheets.

#9 After Dark/BravoCon Live Tickets

The late-night event tickets! After your busy day of BravoCon is over, there is more to do on Saturday night. Bravo typically has a big event planned, and you can attend with another ticket purchase. These are late-to-be-sold tickets, they are extra paid add-ons and for your BravoCon fanatics, it's worth the purchase! So, save up a bit; they are a bit spendy. More to come about these, but they are sold later on, closer to the event!

#10 Photo Ops

While these photo ops are an add-on to all ticket holders, you still have to register on the app to meet your Bravoleb of choice. Bravo releases the photo ops schedule maybe 3 weeks before BravoCon. I believe they wait until the end due to scheduling all the Bravolebs and making sure everyone has fulfilled other commitments with the Bravo Bazaar and Panels, etc.

#11 Wristbands

This is the actual biggest prep event of BravoCon—when wristbands are sent! Everyone waits to get theirs, and the posts in the Facebook group go wild! It's when BravoCon feels real. Just don't put it on early and tighten it!

After wristbands, it's just figuring out everything else personal for your trip! I do believe that Bravo is building on so much more for the event. This chapter, I'm guessing, will stay the same, but I have huge hopes that more is coming for us. Give us everything, take our money!

CHAPTER 4

THE GAME PLAN

I titled this "Game Plan," but really, it's "Your Game Plan." Previously, I discussed the announcement schedule, and now I'm adding it on your prep list for everything else. At some point, this will all mesh together, but if you're prepping, you might as well have the full list (or everything I can think of, at least). If you're an early subscriber and reading now in real time, as I publish, you might want to read again after ticket sales are announced so you can recap. I am writing the book in order of how things happen, so preparation is the beginning step!

The non-Bravo announcement preparation tasks are what I'm covering here. All of these topics will be mentioned again in the book down the line and more in-depth.

Planning Your Time Away Wisely

You will want to be sure you have enough time off of your real life for this. If your work is strict about time off or you can't get all the time off to do the full 3-day weekend, many others have got one-day tickets, and they say they got everything they wanted out of the one-day experience. Since you don't know about your life in six-ten months, use this information as you need.

During BravoCon, you won't have much time to do anything if you're 100% invested. I barely had time to check my work email. At the hotel I was so exhausted and still busy doing things outside the hotel. At night, you'll be out doing other events, and in the morning, you may not get much sleep-in time as the event starts early!

I work for myself, and I did schedule time off from Wednesday until the next Tuesday. I need the morning of Wed to final pack and prep for my flight. In 2022, I came home on Monday but needed Tuesday off to relax. I'm not even kidding; if you think you can go back to work on Tuesday, even if you work from home, you might want to reconsider. Your body, brain, voice, legs, everything is going to need some serious TLC. Just a pro tip!

Even though covid isn't such a concern these days, I made sure the week before BravoCon I wasn't around anyone closely. I wasn't going to risk it. I had too much time and money invested, and as I run the group, I didn't want to risk getting sick and ruining all my good times ahead, no thanks. Just a tip, my B's. It's up to you, of course, to do what you want to do!

Decide When You Want to Fly in/Arrive in Las Vegas

When you're ready to book those flights, keep this in mind... Vegas is a 24-hour entertainment circus, so you have plenty of options for getting affordable flights in. I know of some who come on Wednesday to have time to relax and do other Vegas things. I know someone who flew in on Sunday morning, had the whole day VIP, and flew home at night. Talk about a 24-hour turn and burn!

When you decide your life calendar and when you're coming, have those dates in mind when it comes to buying tickets. There are so many options; literally, you can do anything you want and create the most awesome agenda for yourself.

Since I manage the FB group and need a bit more prep time, I fly in on Wednesdays, relax a bit, get comfy, and figure out the hotel. I booked the LINQ again this year, so I don't need that time to figure out the hotel, but I need pre-game time!! It's my big extravaganza and I love that extra day. This year, I'm going out scootering more than last year. I think I was more nervous as I didn't know the LINQ very well. Keep in mind that we do our big group meetup on Thursday nights. If you want to attend, be sure to fly in on Thursday to make it.

I also had a mess-up in 2023. I thought I was going to need all day Monday to relax and wind down, but I had a change of heart on Sunday. I had some really horrible flights home from Vegas, 2 legs and a long wait at the airport, a bus ride, and then a taxi. I would have been getting home on Wednesday at 3:00 am! I took a loss on my return ticket and rebooked a new flight on Monday, and it got me home Monday night around 10:00 PM. I am so happy I did that; I needed more time to sleep, relax, unpack, and give myself a day off.

Decide What Hotel Is Right for You

As you know, Bravo TV has sent out the links for their hotel group rates, and most, if not all, are sold out already. The hotels still have rooms available; just know the pricing will change frequently, and as that week is an event, the hotels close to the Forum might have higher rates closer to the event time. At the time of writing this, you can't even book a night in for November. When you can, I would definitely book the nights you want. Hotels are covered in Chapter 15.

Decide on How Much Money You Will Need for Food

Do you really need to eat at BravoCon? Some say no, but I say yes, and you should, lol. The people who said no may have said so because they don't have time to eat, or they're so involved in the activities that they don't think of food. I can't deny that. I didn't think of food either. How could I when I had a constant cocktail in hand?

Bravo has some complimentary food at the event for the VIP lounge and some for sale at the Bravo Bazaar outside in the photo ops. Still, plan a budget for food if you're on a budget. I'll chat about food more in Chapter 15.

Decide on How Much Money You Will Need for Vegas Transportation

Transportation in Vegas is not that expensive from my experience last year. I try to support taxis and cabs as opposed to using Uber and Lyft. My reasoning? They are faster at the airport and have flat fee rates. I also have heard from the old school taxi and cab drivers that they can't compete with Lyft and Uber. I try to help support them for this reason too. Other than rides to the airport and back, I didn't take any other paid transportation during my time there. If you don't know, I have a scooter as I'm disabled so it was a bit of fun scooting around Vegas.

Decide on How Much Money You Will Need for Extras/Drinks/Gambling

Oh, the extra fun stuff! If you are a partier and gambler, Vegas serves free drinks when you're gambling, so that's a huge win for you, B's. If you're not into gambling, then expect to have a bit of a bill at the bars when you order drinks. Almost every night, we were at a bar. I can't say drinks were that crazy, but again, it's the time of your life, so plan on having a big bar bill! And yes, you can drink openly anywhere in Vegas!

Decide on Extras/Glam/Makeup/Hair in Vegas

I gave in for 2023 and got my hair done. I felt it was a treat for myself for killing it with the prep of BravoCon. It was well worth it! I think I paid $55 for a wash and blowout. I kept the style for the whole weekend. I should have done a bit more, but as the weekend got away from me, I cared less about it! No joke. Sunday was the "whatever day," and I look back at my old pics with regret. I think it was my first year in Vegas. I was so tired. I just wanted to play as is.

But for you, you might want full glam and need to have that budget, too!

One Final Important Decision, Are You Going Alone or With Friends?

The reason I made the BravoCon Facebook Group was so I could go with other online friends. I made plenty of online friends that year and still to this day! If you don't have any friends or family wanting to go and you still do, please prepare to go solo but don't worry, so many go alone and have the time of their life. Many also connect in the BravoCon Facebook group before the event to have a buddy system!

CHAPTER 5

BRAVOCON
BUDGETS FOR THE B'S

Exactly what the newbies have been looking for and I'm going to get right into it! Many people join the BravoCon Facebook Group prior to the ticket announcement, and they all wonder about this: How much is BravoCon? Well, my B's, it can be very affordable and very expensive. This all depends on how much time you want to spend at the event, how many extras you want to purchase, what ticket type you want, and, of course, all the Vegas and Queen things! I'll run down a list of everything I can think of and discuss options.

BravoCon is an amazing experience and does come with a heavier price tag than most conventions. Everyone has their reasoning on why, but here is why I think it's more costly: the talent. They all have to be paid and their expenses have to be taken care of, including hotels, flights, food, handlers, etc. Last year, I believe 140 Bravolebs attended, and you saw them literally everywhere. Not all conventions have 140 stars from a TV network attend, show up, and are on their feet for 3 days+. Not to mention all the extras for filming, activations, and security. It's quite a bit more.

First, Ticket Talk! (we are not on #ticketwatch yet!)

In 2019 and 2022, there were three ticket options. In 2023, there were two options, so I will say that's what is most likely for the upcoming events. But then again, Bravo might add on an SVIP ticket option again, and of course, those will be hard to get and most definitely expensive. It's well worth it for those who want that experience, though. I also think that everyone dreams of VIP tickets, but keep in mind that those sell out very quickly, so thankfully, Bravo has many other options you can purchase to still have the best experience without a VIP ticket.

Later in the book, I'll review all experiences more in-depth. For now, this is just about planning and budgeting. I'll also add that the prices will most likely be higher due to more BravoCon being added to the experience. So far, each year, the prices have gone up, so expect it.

GA Tickets are "General Admission" or "General Access"

- **3-day GA tickets were sold for $550 without taxes and fees.** This is the most everyone-can-go price but does not come with special privileges. However, you can still enjoy the entire event at a lesser cost, You can use my tips to enjoy the event and have the time of your life! There is plenty you can do and as you read through the book, I'll let you know some secrets on how to meet Bravolebs in "non-traditional" ways. I have kept notes from all the comments in my Facebook Group.

- **1-day GA tickets were sold for $250 without taxes and fees**. This was a popular choice for those who wanted to attend for only one day and experience it all. It's the perfect choice for those who want to have other Vegas experiences. You can do and see many other shows and events. It is a bonus to your trip! This was also a popular choice for those late-to-the-party purchasers; they bought Fri/Sat, and Sunday 1-day passes from different people selling their tickets in the BravoCon Facebook Group.

VIP Tickets are "Very Important Partygoers" (well, it is a 3-day party!)

- **3-day VIP tickets last year were sold for $1200.** This is the Grand Dame of tickets. It gives you better seats for the panels, shorter lines, early purchase for the add-ons, and access to the VIP lounge. The most popular to want to buy, the hardest to purchase. There are limited amounts available, and they go very fast on sale day.
- **1-day VIP were $475.** A great deal for those who want to have a full Vegas experience and do a day of BravoCon. I heard this so many times last year at the event and in the Facebook Group. It was almost perfect.

With only two ticket options, you have many ways to mesh and mix up your ticket choices with your trip planning to Vegas.

Next up! Add-ons

Bravopalooza $260 without taxes and fee.

It's a 1.5-hour more intimate event in a small meetup room at the Forum, a nice add-in for those who want to experience meeting more Bravolebs and photo ops. If you're a GA ticket holder, this is like a small VIP lounge experience.

BravoCon Live.

These are all at night and at the Paris hotel hosted by Bravo (2023)

- The Bravos - Friday, November 3rd @ 9 pm -Mezzanine is $300 +taxes and fees, Orchestra is $400 +taxes and fees
- BravoCon LIVE with Andy Cohen! Charming House Rules - Saturday, November 4th @ 7 pm – Mezzanine is $200 +taxes and fees, Orchestra is $250 +taxes and fees
- BravoCon LIVE with Andy Cohen! Dynamic Duos - Saturday, November 4th @ 10 pm - Mezzanine is $200 +taxes and fees, Orchestra is $250 +taxes and fees
- BravoCon LIVE with Andy Cohen! Bravo's Showgirls - Sunday, November 5th @ 6 pm -Mezzanine is $200 +taxes and fees, Orchestra is $250 +taxes and fees
- BravoCon LIVE with Andy Cohen! The Reading Room - Sunday, November 5th @ 9 pm - Mezzanine is $200 +taxes and fees, Orchestra is $250 +taxes and fees

BravoCon After Dark $449:

A one-night special event hosted by Bravo offsite last year, the After Dark was at the Caesars Hotel. Each year, the talent changes and the Bravolebs attend.

Vegas Hotels:

For your budget, this all depends on how glamorous a hotel you want, the amenities, the proximity to the Forum, and so many things to consider. Of course, when you fly in and leave also affects this, but I say plan on $250 per night for an average hotel.

Approx $1000 for 4 nights if you fly in Thursday and leave Monday.

Flights to Vegas:

These can be super cheap or super expensive, depending on where you live, so I'll leave your flight budget up to you to figure it out. I know of some members in the group that got a flight for $79! I'll just say $300/economy is a good guess. Approx $300

Taxis/Ubers:

A taxi to your hotel and from the hotel to your airport is approximately $30-$40. I paid $30 for each of mine and, of course, a tip extra. Approx $80 with tip

Food at BravoCon

It doesn't matter what ticket you have for BravoCon. At some point, you will need to eat, and while many of us talked about not eating much, you do have to eat. There is some hot food served in the Bravo Bazaar—hamburgers, chicken strips, and some healthy options. The food is a bit higher priced than normal, but overall, if you're just eating for fuel, it's not expensive. I'll talk about food more in Chapter 15. I do remember having a cheeseburger in my scooter for most of the afternoons so I could have quick bites. That's how food wasn't even on my mind! Approx $75 for the 3 days

Drinks:

At BravoCon, the drinks are definitely not cheap. I believe $25 was the average for a cocktail, and that should include tip. Don't quote me on this, though. This is for budgeting purposes. The question is, how many drinks do you plan on having? This is a no-judgment zone, but I'm pretty sure that I had plenty to drink each day! If you plan on having some drinks, that expands the budget! I had drinks at the event and each night.

Merch

I didn't buy any merch but it's not cheap at BravoCon! If you have a love for the Bravoleb merch and having them sign it and all that, expect up to $100 for a starting point. I believe I saw some under $100 but these Bravolebs have a lot going on with their tables/people to run it, costs, shipping, etc. This is why everything is more expensive. I don't think I can give a budget on this but what the heck. $200

Totals

If you are going all in with as much as you can buy and spend, you can expect to spend up to $5000, give or take. BravoCon is like going to Disney World in many aspects. My total last year was $6000, and I had a few extras like a rented scooter and some other things I needed. I didn't gamble much but did eat at Vanderpump Gardens, had drinks, etc.

$6000??? Yep! I'm not the only one who spent that either. Many of us in the poll I took in the Facebook group voted, and that was the average for the high spenders.

Budget-friendly BravoCon B's

I don't even know where to start with this one, but you will need a 3-day GA ticket, flight, hotel, and food at a minimum. There are some crafty ideas you can do to save money, especially with hotels, food, and such. I'm going to say, at a minimum, you should plan on spending $2205. I went through my list and took off some extras, of course.

If you're saving up right now, try to save $125 a month for this for the budget-friendly B's. If you're a high-spender, then plan on saving $333 a month. Is it worth it? If you're a serious Bravo fan and want to do everything extra, YES! It's not just going; it's a 3+ day weekend of pure joy.

CHAPTER 6

WHAT TO EXPECT WHEN YOU BUY A BRAVOCON TICKET

B's, now the big decision! After talking about budgeting, we can talk about how to spend that budget! I know that many B's already have their heart set on VIP and that's their only mission on this BravoCon quest. Last year, I read many comments in our Facebook Group from members who bought GA tickets and had hopes of upgrading. Many got their wish with some good detective work. Chapter 13 covers selling and buying tickets in-depth, but until then, let's talk about what you get with each ticket.

There is a big difference between a GA ticket and a VIP ticket. I'll explain all the options and why, for some, it doesn't make a difference—the experience is still amazing!

Taken off the Bravocon2023 site and edited for easy reading
All ticket holders receive:

- Access to BravoCon for all three days of the event; and it includes the Bravo Live stage, Glam, panels, etc. Once you are in the Forum, unless it's a paid add-on or VIP access, you can pretty much do everything else. And once you are in, be sure to check out the Forum. I found a few fun rooms that I didn't know about!

- Access to Bravo Bazaar; this is where all the Merch, food sales, other vendors, and activations are.

- Access to Bravo-themed and Bravoleb photo ops, both inside and outside.

- Access to all food and beverage options, both inside and outside.

GA

- Option to purchase tickets to Add-On Experiences, including evening shows (pending availability). Last year, Bravo had some extra tickets after the VIPs had their option to buy, so that could happen again.

VIP

- VIP fast lane at Caesars Forum entrance: There are usually two velvet-roped areas when you go to a scheduled event. GA has a longer line, and VIP has a shorter line.

- Preferred seating at BravoCon programming at Caesars Forum, typically in the front rows.

- Access to VIP-exclusive lounge spaces. I'm guessing it might change again, as it did change quite a bit from 2022 to 2023.
- VIP access to Bravo-themed and Bravoleb photo ops; this is where the VIP ticket is worth it. The lines for the photo ops can be very long; the VIP line is much shorter.
- VIP fast lane access to all bars (for 21+ attendees). There is a VIP bar in the Bravo Bazaar, and it's roped off, so it is faster to get drinks. However, I frankly had more fun getting drinks in the bazaar's open area and talking to people in line! Good place to catch up on gossip and what's going on. Just like on the shows, there is drama sometimes at BravoCon!
- Early access option to purchase tickets to Add-On Experiences, including evening shows (pending availability).
- Priority entry to special add-on experiences with purchased ticket (pending availability).

In 2023, we saw many changes in terms of event space, making the long lines to get into the panels not even worth complaining about. All the panel rooms were very large and had plenty of seating. I read so many posts in the Facebook Group from those who bought GA, and they all had a great time. So, if you decide to skip VIP to spend your money on other fabulous queen things (drinks, merch, eating out, gambling, etc.), you're on a great track. A weekend in Vegas is such a great experience; you can do so many more things!

Remember, there are so many crafty ways to change your tickets after you buy them. Either way, buy tickets on sale day and figure out the swaps later on. Also, if you miss tickets on sale day, many members get tickets later on, so don't give up hope. In fact, some still went to Vegas and got wristbands that day! The Bravo family is so giving and helpful. You will find that our members of the group are the best at selling tickets within our group! I'll cover safe buying and selling in Chapter 13.

Will SVIP Make A Comeback?

BravoCon organizers are known for switching things up every BravoCon. With 2024 being a "pause year," I hope the event team will review all of the attendee feedback we all gave and bring back SVIP. The fanbase will definitely buy them. However, as I write this, I don't know what they would change up as last year, in 2023, the two ticket options seemed appropriate for the event.

Here are some final questions to keep in mind when you get to buy the tickets, especially if you are new to BravoCon:

- Budget
- What other events do you want to do while you're in Vegas? Is BravoCon part of a larger trip to Vegas? Do you want to see other shows, events, and have other adventures?
- Do you want VIP lounge and shorter line access? (I think these are the two most valuable perks of the VIP ticket)
- Do you want to attend all three days?
- Would you prefer to do a mix-up of tickets, like one day GA and two days VIP or two days GA and one day VIP?

Newbies, there are so many decisions to make, but at least now you know your options. Going to BravoCon and having the full experience is something you've never experienced. I guarantee that.

CHAPTER 7

THE BRAVOCON
EXPERIENCES

It's time to review all the fun stuff in detail of all the experiences you can have at BravoCon. This is all based on my past experiences and what I have read from the members in the group. Personally, I didn't do them all because I chose not to attend some of them. You have the freedom to choose what interests you, and you'll figure out what you want to do once you get your tickets, organize your Bravoleb list, and check the schedules. It's important to have your list ready to build your own schedule.

Last year, we were all new to the Forum, so finding our way around was part of the fun. There was so much go find and figure out. No one knew what they were doing, and I recall so many conversations with people saying, "I saw her at this stage, and he was at that stage." Even with a strict schedule, you can still get distracted by the next fun thing going on that comes your way. A 3-day carnival? That's what it should say on the ticket; it's definitely like a 3-day Bravo carnival! You never know what Bravoleb is going to be attending and who you will see, so expect a few unexpected detours that happen—all happy mistakes! That's how I went last year. I only had a few photo ops scheduled and a Bravopalooza, and that's it. I wanted the rest to be a Bravo playland for myself. I know of many, though, that have a full spreadsheet full of all-day events scheduled, and they hit each event as they had an agenda of people they wanted to hear speak, get photo ops with, or enjoy an experience.

Bravo Bazaar

Think of this as the ultimate meeting place for everything—kind of an open market, a place where everyone with any ticket can go and mingle around. This is the huge main room of the Forum that is right in front of the entrance doors. You really can't miss it. It has maybe 5 doors from the front to enter and 2 on the right side (Next to the big hallway).

Vendors:

Inside, you will find vendors offering fun activities and activations all catered to us, and most of them are Bravo-themed. It's fun to go around and see what they are doing. The marketing people take this seriously and have some fun giveaways or marketing swag for you to take with you. All the major sponsors of the event have the biggest spots, and of course, Jake from State Farm has showed up twice. It's kinda fun to see him taking selfies with everyone.

Food:

In the back of the Bazaar is the food area with simple offerings such as burgers, chicken strips, snacks, fruit, and such. It's not too expensive but everyone collectively talked about the food as not the best. I have to be honest about that so you will know what to expect. I did go through the food line and got a cheeseburger. I figured it would fill me up to drink more all day and fuel me for the afternoon. I ate breakfast at my hotel prior and started my first cocktail at 10:00 am, so by early afternoon, I was ready for a protein bomb.

The lines were kind of long (went quickly), but there were not many complaints as everyone in line was having fun laughing and talking about their favorite topic, BRAVO. There are some areas to sit to eat, so you can sit down and enjoy the food. If you're not into this type of food, then you best plan for other options for yourself. Leaving the Forum to eat during this event is not something I heard anyone say. Once you are in, you are there for the day!

I may have missed some of the food in the Bazaar, but that's my recollection of it. By that point, I was a bit tipsy because my fun is scooting around, a drink in my scooter cup, enjoying the day.

Merch:

There is so much merch, and it delivers! If you love your Bravoleb merch, this is the place to buy it. Many of the Bravolebs have their own booth and do show up at random times to help promote and sell the items they have for sale. This changes every year, so expect it. Bravolebs are Reality TV stars, and for some, this is their career. Having merch at the event is important for their own brand, so if you're planning on buying their merch before the event online, you'll probably pay a lower price than in person.

If you wait to buy merch in person, there is a good chance you can meet the Bravoleb, have them sign your items, get a picture or video, and have a longer conversation. They love interacting with fans, having an exchange about them or the show or how you feel, so bring that excitement when you want to meet your favorite Bravoleb for sure!

Pricing... Expect a higher price tag for this, as it's a specialty purchase at this point. Many members in the group mentioned the higher price tag, but the experience of meeting the Bavolebs is worth it (especially if you caught them at their booth like I did with Caroline Stanbury). Would I have bought a horrible human bag online? No, but does having Caroline sign one for me and now having it hanging in my Bravo Studio have a different feeling? Absolutely. It was $20, well worth it, and so fun.

Keep in mind that many of them have to pay for the booths, pay for staff, pay for shipping their merch, pay for anything else they bring to decorate, and all that. That's why the pricing is higher; everything at BravoCon costs money to do.

The most fun thing about the Merch booths by Bravolebs is the unpredictability of when Bravolebs will show up at the booth. You may wander up and down a row and not see any. The next minute, you see one shuffling in, and their booth is completely stacked with a line of everyone waiting. There is no official schedule; it's just one of those things you have to wait for between your other events, but an insider tip: ask the people running the booth when they will be back. They might tell you, so you know when to come back! The Bravolebs all have schedules for their busy day, so get there early and wait it out. You won't be alone.

If you are a GA ticket holder, this is huge, an open event to meet, greet, and snap pics. Some Bravolebs are still open to talking and meeting you without buying their merch. Some do have a roped area, and only people who buy their merch can do a photo op. But you can take close-up pictures of them either way, as it's an open area.

The merch area is in the middle of the main Forum area. The food is behind it, as well as a lot of black curtain areas.

Bars:

There were two bars in the Bazaar area last year. I only went to one, but I recall two. I went to the one closest to the right-side entrance as it was by the big hallway on the right side of the Forum. They had a few bartenders and two different sides open with lines, not all the time though. Remember, lines all depend on what is going on during that time. If you get there when a big panel is going on, the lines might be shorter. After a panel, expect a long line. One thing Bravo did was organize differently in 2023; they had it all figured out from 2022 for sure.

Pricing? It's Vegas. Expect a cocktail to be much higher than where you live. Expect to pay event pricing and tip accordingly.

Specialty cocktails are available for faster service. You can order any drink, though, and the common cocktails, like Jack/Coke, are also available. You don't have to drink from the drink menu. They make a themed drink, and it's fun to order the "Whoop it up" as many of us did! I think a cocktail was $18 or so. With a tip, it's approximately $21. I will be honest; the lines were not that long that you needed to order a double. I had a member from the group buy me a drink and get me a double that was $48! It knocked the Bravo out of me. I regretted that!

Activations

The unexpected fun of BravoCon! Each year, the team introduces many new experiences that come with any ticket. In 2019, those who weren't at the event and watching in the Facebook BravoCon Group were so excited to watch them and somewhat experience them online. It was amazing! The first one I remember was short videos you could make having that look/feel of pouring drinks at Sur and holding a golden apple of RYONY. The videos are in slow motion and have the music of your favorite show. It's really a fun time to have them made, and they email them to you so you can watch and share. Again, all are included in both GA and VIP tickets.

I won't get into details on this as I don't know what they are doing for the upcoming events, but there are many of them, so when you plan your time for the Bravo Bazaar, plan on doing them. They are worth it! You can do these alone or with a group of friends!

Bravoland is a favorite for many. It's a historical tour of your favorite Bravo shows with props, as well as other things on display. You can do photo ops of yourself in the "sets" of Below Deck, Summer House, WWHL clubhouse with the shotski, and many more. I admit, I didn't get to it in 2023. I did go in 2022, but honestly, I was chasing down my favorite Bravoleb and didn't "experience" it as I should have. I had a 9:30 am photo op with Bravoleb and heard they were in Bravoland. I went looking for them, but sadly, I didn't find them, so I went back to the photo op. In 2022, Bravoland was in an area I didn't go back to, so I didn't see it.

VIP Lounge

If you have a VIP ticket and see the main bar in the Bazaar with a long line, you can hit up the VIP lounge in the Bazaar. In 2023, it was placed in a roped-off area on the right side of the room. I never saw a line, so this is one of the fast-tracked bonuses for a VIP ticket holder. They don't sell food but have some snacks available for purchase, such as a baby charcuterie tray in a package. Again, nothing fancy but a quick bite to fill you up with some protein. They also have some loungey, comfy seats and couches to relax a bit—a huge bonus to give your little busy feet a break.

Reminder: Every VIP event or area has security looking for the wristband. The VIP Lounge in the Bazaar also requires a wristband for entry. There are no Bravolebs in the lounge, but it's a great place to get faster service, sit, and hang out.

Final Question

Are Bravolebs just walking around the Bazaar? Yes and no. The A+ list Bravolebs are most likely not going to be walking around, but you might run into other cast members of a show that was on a season just wandering around. We saw a few of them in 2022, like Dave the Chef from Below Deck. He got a lot of selfies of him posted in our group. Members were so surprised to see him out in the wild. He was so nice to everyone and took all the selfies. I saw him myself a few times, and I felt for him; he experienced his first Bravoleb alone, not knowing what was going to happen to him, lol!

The Bravo Bazaar was such a large room it never felt crowded. You can walk around without being in a large crowd and sit and enjoy some downtime. I really felt like it was a place to hang out during the event. It's the marketplace of BravoCon. Expect to make this your one-stop shop for everything for any ticket holder! Photo ops, buy merch, eat, drink, participate in activations, and relax your little footies when you need a break!

CHAPTER 8

THE BRAVOCON EXPERIENCES: BRAVOPALOOZA

W hen you buy your ticket to BravoCon, be prepared to start adding more experiences to your schedule for the weekend. As I have mentioned before, some add-ons are free, and some are paid. Bravopalooza is one of those paid experiences, but well worth it if you want to make the most of your time there. This experience is also one of the first to get released for sale after GA and VIP tickets are sold. Expect to wait for a few weeks to a month. They might go on sale much later, depending on when they start selling tickets.

I'll start with costs. As I didn't go in 2019, I don't remember the prices, but in 2022, they were $165, I believe (I might be wrong; I didn't buy any that year), and in 2023, $262 (including fees and taxes). I bought one from another member of the

BravoCon Facebook group. With the new venue, costs in 2023 went up a lot from 2022. I'll close with how to swap and buy/sell Bravopalooza tickets safely.

After I go into detail about Bravopalooza, you can then decide if you want to add this to your budget planning. Many people buy as many as they can, and some are happy doing one or two the entire weekend.

The Experience

When you arrive at the room scheduled for your Bravopalooza, you will already feel a bit special. There are red velvet ropes to separate the GA and VIP lines, and they should not be too long, as there are limited tickets sold. If you arrive really early, you will get closer to the front, and then you have to just wait. There are no benches or seats, so prepare to stand for a while. During the wait, the hallway is usually full of excitement, making it a great time to chat it up with others. When the current Bravopalooza is ending, the Bravolebs will come out the same doors you are going in, so you get to see them a bit up close and can take some pictures. Last year, I was in a room that was close to another event, so we got to see even more Bravolebs as time passed. It was so much fun just being in the hallway!

Once the doors open, you get to walk in and see luxury décor and servers hand-delivering hors d'oeuvres, high-top tables to group up with friends, and some comfortable seating around the entire room. There is one main bar to get your cocktails (in 2023, you also got 2 drink tickets; I am not sure if they will continue). I also believe some of the servers were offering some themed cocktails or champagne. You'll find it to feel like a more intimate room, but expect it to be full of people mingling around for the entire time.

When you look around, you'll also see the photo ops area where the Bravolebs will do the meet and greet and take pictures. They have a nice big backdrop with that "Hollywood" feeling. There are two small stages for photo ops with two different sets of Bravolebs. Most were paired with someone from their show, but not always. In fact, when you buy your ticket, you don't know who you are even going to see at your scheduled time! Bravo keeps this a mystery ticket. Interesting twist, huh? These experiences are 1.5 hours, and if you want to buy more cocktails, you certainly can.

I had two Bravopalooza tickets in 2023: Kyle Richards and Heather Dubrow. I was so excited to meet them both at the same time. I felt like I hit the jackpot! The quick conversation I had with Kyle was actually about a member of her family in our Facebook BravoCon group, and Kyle laughed and said, "I don't doubt it. I have so many cousins!". Heather looked so absolutely stunning that I don't even remember what I said to her, lol!

One cool thing that happened was just randomly seeing other non-Housewives just walking around, talking to everyone, and mingling in the crowd. Suzy and I took a break to sit and chat a bit in the corner by a plant and charged up my scooter, and, lo and behold, Riley from Below Deck came right up to us and started chatting. I barely recognized her! She looked so muscular and strong on the show that when I saw her in a cocktail dress (total fox!), my mind was blown, especially by the fact that she came up to us! It was truly one of the highlights of my entire three days at BravoCon, the random, unexpected surprises!

Then, next up, while sitting in the same spot next to the plant, there is Luis and Tre, and Captain Glenn just walking around talking to us, too! I had already met Luis and Tre at another photo op, so this round of chatting was more about just fun stuff. I know they get a lot of heat on social media, but I did enjoy the conversation I had with both of them. I now think I recall seeing some Bravolebs sitting on the couch just hanging out, too. Of course, these were not A-list, but you'd recognize them if you saw them. Like Brooks Marks! Suzy grabbed me and said, "Lisa, it's Brooks." He was just mingling around also by the plant! He was probably a bit shy, but we dragged him to our gossip corner. This was all in the same Bravopalooza, by the way!

Bravolebs

Most Bravolebs scheduled for BravoCon will participate in Bravopalooza for photo ops or just mingle around. Again, you won't know until you get there. What if you don't like some of the Bravolebs at the photo ops? Well, that happened to me. I didn't want to meet this one "star" of a West Coast hot show, so I just stayed next to the plant and watched the room. That in itself was fun! Yep, I, too, just like you, might not like all the Bravolebs. Can you guess that I liked sitting by that plant? Luckily for me, many of the members in our group were there, and we all chatted about the other things going on. So, if you see me there sitting by myself on the scooter, come say hi! I actually sat there because the room was packed, and I couldn't scoot around that easily.

Food and Drinks

The hors d'oeuvres were special for the event and not offered anywhere else but in the Bravopalooza rooms. Don't expect it to be filling, but it was a nice snack during the day. The drink tickets did offer what was on the list off the menu, but they were nice and strong. BravoCon does not let you down with watered-down cocktails.

Lounge Feels

Yep, this experience does have the comfortable lounge feeling, even though the lines for the photo ops might seem to get in the way in some of the rooms, you can grab a couch and talk amongst friends. And some are not at full capacity either. It all depends on how many show up! Some members missed their Bravopalooza, and I admittingly missed one start time and ended up missing the whole thing!

Photo Ops

Long lines are a possibility, and the rooms are not that big, so it won't be too long to get the photo op. I noticed that when one photo op is busy, the other might be empty until the first one slows down, then both run simultaneously.

The VIP line is only for entry. I don't recall a VIP line inside, but there might have been one. I had to get special help due to my scooter, so I didn't really notice that. If you are disabled, Bravo and their security do an A+ job of helping you get in and out of the photo ops quickly. I found the staff so sincere and caring to make sure we all have the same advantages as everyone else. I think it also helps them with traffic in the room, as it can get crowded if a scooter gets stuck in a line. Having people getting around me could have been a bit worrisome. However, I had no issues whatsoever. So, if you're disabled and unsure about attending, there's no need to worry!

You also can have someone else take your pictures with your phone, and the staff will take the pictures as well for you if you want. They usually take a lot of pictures very fast, so you have options, but prepare for one thing—there's no time to decide! These photo ops are quick, and they keep the line moving. While quick, you still can have a minute or two to chat with the Bravoleb. They are not rushing you, but there is a line, so keep that in mind when you're having your minute with your favorite Bravoleb.

That about wraps up the experience. I had two photo ops last year; one I missed, and then I had this fab one I discussed. Don't miss it! Be sure to have your schedule ready and be ready for any surprises, including running into Bravolebs before and after your photo ops in the lines in the hallway. You might just see Andy in the hallway like I did in 2023. He was walking right at me, and yep, I got a selfie with him! Andy is everywhere at BravoCon!

Ticket Sales and Swaps

Bravo TV sells these tickets and then some other websites will sell them too for a much higher price. They arrive via email with a QR Code to get in. Be sure to print this as well and have it very handy on your phone for entrance. I print everything, by the way. You never know if your phone is going to have issues before the event.

If you miss out on the first round sold by Bravo and don't want to pay the high prices from other outlets, the BravoCon Facebook Group offers a safer place to buy and sell these. It is all about trust, though. However, in my years of running this group, I haven't heard any reports of anyone being sold a scam ticket for this add-on experience. You do need to do a few things first:

Selling and Buying

Post in the group if you have tickets for sale. Any tickets not taken by the members on my waitlist can be sold in the group. You must show your receipt with your name on it. Your name must match your Facebook profile. Our mod team will then go through your Facebook profile to make sure they are a real person. Once we determine you're real, we will approve the post. You cannot sell for any more than what you paid; this is a firm rule we have. Most people were not able to attend either changed their mind about an add-on or can't go to BravoCon at all. We are a family, and we help each other.

Our group members are well-trained to report anyone in the comments trying to sell outside of our rules and guidelines, and that person is immediately removed, no questions asked. You will find the group's loyalty very strong. It's a great feeling to know everyone has each other's backs.

Once you post and you find someone who wants to buy the Bravopalooza tickets, we have guidelines on that, too. We recommend a Facebook video or Facetime with the buyer/seller to make sure it's a real person. I have heard so many stories of two Bs in the group having the best time talking about BravoCon and sharing why they can't go or whatever. I just love our group!!!

Then the decision on how to do the financial transactions is next. Most choose Venmo as it's easy, while some opt for PayPal due to the transaction type. After you make the payment, the seller will email you the QR Code, and then it's all yours. Again, this is a lot of trust, but we have these guidelines for safer buying/selling for a reason.

One request I have is this: please do not message me asking if someone is a scammer. I will immediately reply "YES" because of the firm rules everyone knows about. If you're being approached directly, it's likely a scam. And again, from another group, probably! Responsible members only sell through the approached methods we know work.

CHAPTER 9

THE BRAVOCON EXPERIENCES: PHOTO OPS

The photo ops is probably the most popular of all the experiences at BravoCon because everyone wants photos of their favorite Bravolebs and themselves! If you are new to BravoCon, I'll fill you in on everything I know about the photo ops, but be ready; Bravo loves to change things up, as I've mentioned. we might have the same or a whole new photo ops-type event or more!

After tickets go on sale, the other tickets will be sold in order, and then follows the big information we all die for—the Bravolebs attending. Once that is out, next up should be the photo ops. In 2023, it was announced about 5 weeks before BravoCon. Again, mostly to have a guaranteed show of the Bravolebs. You will get the photo ops schedules in your mobile app, so check it as soon as it's updated because they will book out quickly! Remember, this is a no-fee experience!

In 2022, I scheduled only one photo op. I didn't know how it all worked, and I was so busy managing the Facebook Group that I figured I'd meet enough Bravolebs. 2022 was crazy. After two years of no BravoCon, we were wild with anticipation! During that time, though, I was very thrilled to meet that one "Bravoleb" I had a crush on. I was so excited. It was my first year, and I didn't know much about how photo ops worked.

In 2023, they had an entire tent for the photo ops. This was a game-changer! We didn't know at the time when the schedule was released that there would be a tent outside just for photo ops or how big the experience was going to be! We didn't know anything, actually because BravoCon had never held at the Forum until then. We all got to experience this together.

The Mobile App Schedule

When you get the app and see who is doing the photo ops, you might be surprised to find that many Bravolebs are paired up in unexpected ways, not always according to their shows. Bravo does a great job with these pairings, so you can expect to see many Bravolebs from the same shows together. But sometimes, you'll get a delightful surprise with Bravolebs from different shows paired up—double win! (I had Vicki Gunvalson and Heather Dubrow)

I don't recall, but there might have been a limit of two photo ops you could choose from. I believe in 2022 it was unlimited, but that year was a lot different. I heard many in the Facebook Group mention they had gone to so many photo ops. You will see so many Bravolebs during the entirety of the event that I would not worry about only having two photo ops. The event is crawling with Bravolebs, and remember: in the Bazaar you get photos too.

Swapping or Selling Your Photo Ops

There is absolutely no selling of photo ops in the Facebook Group. I did get wind of people trying to sell theirs, and we booted them out as soon as we found them doing this. However, swapping or gifting photo ops is common and permitted for some reasons—people change their minds or have conflicts with other experiences they want to attend. This is, again, all part of the planning for the best time of your life. Coming up, the crazy scheduling!

Photo Ops + 1

Yep, last year, each photo-op allowed you to have another person attend with you. So, each photo op comprised of you two and two Bravolebs. You could just go by yourself, but last year, we found the group was more than happy to share their photo ops with others who really wanted to see one Bravoleb in addition to what they got with their ticket. There will be a post in the group when we are ready to announce that.

In the Photo Op Tent

Last year, the photo ops were outside the back area of the Forum. You will find it when you explore the Forum. There are many exit doors that go to a large outdoor area to walk around and sit on the benches. You can enjoy more cocktails there and find many groups of Bravo fans all talking about the Bravolebs. You will go down a ramp and find the tent. Once inside, you will see a food area to the right and many tables where you can sit, enjoy, and relax while you wait for the photo op. I believe some merch is also sold here, too; the tent is huge!

Then, you will see the roped-off lines for each photo op. They are long, which is why there are tables. Maybe this is why you can bring a friend—one can hold a spot while the other relaxes. Most people just wait in line, though. The lines go faster than you think, but you will have to wait in line. The photo ops are scheduled very tightly, so they only allow so many people per photo op time. It's nice to know this this beforehand so you don't have to show up right on time, but you have to show up during the time of your scheduled photo op.

Should you show up early?

If you come very early, wait at the tables, and get in line asap, then sure! Show up early, and you will be in line sooner. Either way, you will spend time waiting or waiting in line.

More about My Photo Ops Experience

I happened to really enjoy my time in the photo ops area. I only got one photo op for myself, and it was Vicki Gunvalson and Heather Dubrow. I had talked to Vicki before during a live interview, so I was more excited to meet Heather. I was also gifted one photo op from a friend in the group for Emily and Gina. While waiting in line, we saw Terry Dubrow walk past. Anytime I saw a Bravoleb even get near me, I did a huge wave and said their name and they usually stopped to say hi and let me snap a selfie. I found this to be common during the entirety of the event. Don't let a moment pass you by! Remember, some of the Bravo husbands are very close by, just walking around like the rest of us! They are just as accommodating when it comes to pictures and showing excitement. The Bravolebs know that you are all dying to take pictures and meet them, even if just for a quick few seconds during the picture—hugs and very close pictures, too. You'd be surprised how many just want to show their love to the fans!

When I got to the photo op with Emily and Gina, my friend and I got all the pictures, and then I asked Emily about her husband, Shane. She said he was over on the side of the stage, and I should go say hi. I'm a huge fan of Shane. I loved his comeback in the past few seasons, and he was also a member of our Facebook Group, so I had to talk about that! (We have some Bravolebs in the group!)

I went over to Shane and had a great long discussion about him and his love for Emily, the support he gives to the fans and how much he enjoys reading the online commentary about the Housewives of Orange County. We shared so many laughs, and it was amazing to get to spend more than a couple of minutes. Honestly, I cherished this as a super fan.

Then, boom. I turned around from Shane and ran into Ryan, Jen's fiancé from Orange County! I had another great conversation with Ryan, and then Jen showed up. We three had so much fun laughing and just sharing conversation. Another great and unexpected moment I had! We took a bunch of selfies, and then boom, there was Luis and Teresa from New Jersey! They were getting ready to go up to their photo op, so I caught them before.

I was just hanging out with the side-stage people this entire time. I wasn't doing anything wrong; I was not in an area I should not have been, so it was like this secret little hangout space I had for quite a while. While Teresa was on stage, I talked to Luis, and we chatted it up with Ryan. It was wild! I'm not a huge Jersey fan, so I didn't know all the stories of drama going on, but he told me quite a bit, and I was just like a normal person here. He might have enjoyed that I was a normal person and not a super fan of their show. Teresa joined us later, and we all took selfies on stage. I didn't have a photo op for them; it was just a random hangout. There are things that I love sharing, I wasn't anyone special to them—I was just at the right place at the right time thing.

After it was all over, I scooted back inside and resumed partying on. I will never forget that time in the tent. It was one of my favorite memories of BravoCon 2023!

Tips

One tip I heard from others in the group many times over was, "Keep your time with the Bravolebs short." Others want to meet them, too, and you will get respect from the people in line by keeping it short. Take your picture and say something meaningful to them. I tried to think of something unique to say, even though they would most likely not remember. When I met Heather Dubrow at the Bravopalooza, I told her that I had checked out her new Fire app and was considering using it for my platform. At the time, it was something that excited her and sparked a reaction.

Don't expect to get personal contact information unless you mention something to them and they really want to connect with them after the event. I did hear of this happening. However, it depends on what you have to offer. Most will give you their handler details or have you get connected with them, but I wouldn't expect that type of communication.

If you ask them to follow you on social media, they most likely will not have the time during your photo op to do this, and they won't remember. Therefore, I would not advise that you waste your few minutes of time with them asking them this. Still, some Bravolebs might just fall in adornment with you and follow you. Just follow your gut instincts on this one!

You get two photo ops, so remember to get your favorite list ready for the schedule release!

CHAPTER 10

THE BRAVOCON EXPERIENCES: THE PANELS

The information I have for panels is more for the new BravoCon attendees. I don't have a lot to write about as I didn't go to any panels. Still, I have some great info! If you went in the past, you know these typically are the same, but you never know! Bravo might change it up. Reminder: BravoCon is so full of constant activities that you might opt to skip an activation or activity. I skipped the panels because I chose to scoot around and meet members from the BravoCon Facebook Group during that time. Our group had so much fun I wanted to meet them out in the wild!

The Panels

BravoCon offers a sit-down theatre experience for the fans to watch their favorite Bravolebs talk on stage with a guest moderator (usually someone in the BravoVerse or very connected to Bravo shows through their own celebrity or media). I'd really consider these mini-talk shows if you are new to BravoCon and trying to get a feel of what it's like. Usually, these panels are scheduled back-to-back with little to no break in between.

These experiences are typically 30-45 minutes long. Things can get heated at these panels! Each panel has a unique name, and each year, there are new panels, all based on the hot topics since the last BravoCon. Some panels are named after the guests and how it relates to their shows. You may also find some great matchups of many shows all meshed together. Others are just great topics to discuss that have nothing to do with a show and Bravolebs; for example, the producers talking about their show.

This is definitely a popular experience with the attendees. If you are not in the BravoCon Facebook Group, please join and search for "panels" and read up on the past posts about it.

Cost: The panels are another free add-on experience for all ticket holders.

Schedule Release

Last year, the panel schedules were released on the mobile app about 5 weeks before the event. This is not a lot of time to plan, but hopefully, you will be ready to fill in your BravoCon schedule with the panels. Remember, prior to panels release, you should have the Bravopalooza, and other paid add-ons already purchased. Panels and photo ops are free and depend on the Bravolebs who are confirmed to attend, with details released just before the event.

The Lines

There will be lines for the popular panels, so if you really want to attend one, be sure to get in line early. There are VIP and GA lines. If you're late, you won't need to wait in line, of course, but your seating options will be limited when you get inside, and you might have to sit in the back.

Seating

As mentioned, it's like a sit-down theatre. The Forum has a couple of different "stages" and the one panel I saw was in a large room with seating for a few hundred. The VIP ticket holders get the closer seats, and the GA will be seated behind the VIP. Regardless, everyone can see the stage just fine.

Questions

Some of the panels do allow for questions from the audience. It will all depend on the panel, moderators, etc. You'll find out during your panel if you can ask a question, so have one ready if you want to participate!

Meet and Greet

These are not a meet-and-greet experience, so don't plan on walking on stage and meeting the Bravolebs.

Examples of some of the past panels can be found at: https://www.bravotv.com/the-daily-dish/bravocon-2023-saturday-november-4-complete-schedule

Pro Tip: *The bathrooms are very close to the panels. Many people mentioned the long lines for the bathroom after a panel gets out, so if you have something to do right after your panel, try to get to the bathroom beforehand.*

CHAPTER 11

THE BRAVOCON NIGHT EXPERIENCES

Just like Andy's daily nightly WWHL shows, BravoCon also has three different "live audience" shows hosted each night by Andy. Each year seems to have a different theme, and since details for upcoming events are still unknown, we will wait to find out what they are. However, I can give you some information about what to expect.

In 2023, Friday night was the "Bravos," an award show-style theme. I believe it was for about an hour and filmed with breaks. You can see all the cameras and the production team doing their work. It's really exciting, to be honest. It's like a live award show you see on TV. Now, because it's Bravo, of course, it's a bit campy and fun, not serious.

Vicki Gunvalson won the Wifetime Achievement Award. Will they have that again? I would think so, but who would win it? I'm going to go with LuAnn as she has been on since season one of RHONY. Just my guess, though! The awards were super cute and filled with fun Bravolebs all getting on stage doing a small spot. They keep it going fast, so you don't really notice the breaks and cameras and such.

If you can get a ticket for the Friday night show, I recommend going to this one for sure. It's like the kickoff night for the weekend!

Saturday and Sunday night shows were titled "BravoCon Live!" and both nights had a different theme. Just like Bravo, they have a group of Bravolebs, some on the same shows, some on different shows, sometimes doing a game-show style hour or "Squash that beef." This one is a crowd favorite, so I would not be shocked to see it back again. Every BravoCon has different Bravolebs, so you can never tell what creative ideas the production team will come up with.

Paris Theatre

Once you get to the Paris hotel, there are so many restaurants you can visit before the show. Definitely take time and wander around. It's so gorgeous! If you Google the restaurants prior, you can book a reservation early and then hit the show in the theatre after. It's a big night, so whoop it up! Lisa Vanderpump also has "Vanderpump Garden," which you can reserve for the night of the show. These tickets are not put out for public sale until maybe two months before BravoCon, and they will go fast. I recommend trying to get reservations for another time besides right before show time (**Side Story:** Last year, we had reservations on Wednesday night. Of course, we went as soon as I unpacked at the hotel! I had to get my Bravo on and energy going!).

Last year, I took my scooter to the streets of Las Vegas and got to enjoy a beautiful night scooter ride from the LINQ to the Paris Hotel. It was about 20 min or so. We got there a bit early. I wanted to spot out Bravolebs and just hang out a bit. I did see a few of the husbands having drinks in the bar next to the Paris Theatre, but not many people bothered them. I believe I saw Slade and the Jersey Husbands. I'm not 100% sure, but I recall that group of men there. Again, never be shocked if you see a Bravoleb in the wild. They are not famous to everyone in the world. To normal Vegas gamblers, they are just one of us!

After spending time outside of the theatre, it was time to get in line and wait to get in. There was a bar inside the theatre, and we got a cocktail before we went inside the auditorium to get seated. The vibe was much different than the year before at the Manhattan Center. I just love a good NYC feeling at night, but Vegas brings the sexy as well!

Once seated, you have time to just look around and yep, spot Bravolebs just walking in their seats, talking and doing their mingling with others around them. Not many just walk around; it's a seated auditorium.

For me, it's an experience worth paying for. This is an additional fee experience.

Tickets

The Bravos were $300, and the other BravoCon Live tickets were $250. I would expect that to change each year, but that's what we all paid for last year. Tickets are sold by Bravo's ticket handler company.

Buying/Selling off Bravo's site

Sometimes, you buy everything you can when you get the chance, and life happens, or your plans change, and you can't attend after buying tickets. As this is a paid experience, you will see others trying to sell these tickets on StubHub/other ticket websites and, of course, in scam Facebook Groups, other sites online, etc.

Our BravoCon Facebook group has strict rules against overpricing tickets. If you buy tickets and want to make money, go elsewhere. The Bravo family already has a hard time buying tickets, and finding someone to try to make money is not what we are about!

Show Times (2023)

- Friday only has one show, 9:00 PM
- Saturday has two shows, 6:00 PM and 9:00 PM
- Sunday has two shows, 7:30 PM and 10:00 PM

While BravoCon is at the Forum, The Bravos and all the shows are held at the Paris Theatre in the Paris Hotel. I'm guessing it will be in Paris again, but we will find out next year!

Cocktails

Once you enter the theatre, there is a bar where you can purchase cocktails, and yes, you can bring them inside the auditorium. I recommend getting a nice cocktail and watching the show all the way through. It's not a long show, so you might miss some of the fun if you have to go to get a cocktail when the show has started. Also, be sure to get a bathroom break beforehand if you can!

Food

There wasn't any food that I noticed at the bar, so it's best to eat before or after the show.

Getting to the Theatre

- You can walk (weather permitting)! Last year the weather was perfect for a night walk to the theatre!
- Taxi/Cab/Uber/Drive
- Monorail

After the Show

You might see some Bravolebs coming out of the theatre, wandering around! As mentioned, the husbands were just having drinks in the open patio bar outside the theatre. Although it is hard to remember, I think we also saw some walking by. Nevertheless, these are good times to go and hang out if you're on the hunt for Bravolebs in the wild!

CHAPTER 12

THE BRAVOCON VIP LOUNGE AND EXTRAS:

BRAVOLAND, BRAVOCON LIVE STAGE, AND AFTER DARK PARTY

Here is the scoop about the extras: VIP Lounge, BravoLand, BravoCon Live Stage, and After Dark Party.

VIP Lounge

I'll kick off with the most luxurious of rooms, the famous "VIP Lounge." I have discussed lightly the VIP lounge area in the Bravo Bazaar, but the main VIP lounge definitely is deserving of its own section.

The VIP lounge in 2023 was located in the Forum and was on the right side of the building. When you walk into the main entrance of the Forum, take a right, and then at the end of the hallway, take a left, then down the hallway, take a right, and then take a left. No worries, once you find it, you'll navigate yourself there every time with no issues. The room it was held in was very large. In fact, when I first walked in, I was awestruck at how much larger it was than in 2022.

The entry of the lounge has a welcoming area of sorts, and then you can scout the room and see all the luxury your heart has been desiring for all the months of waiting. I'm not going to get into details of the room itself; I'll leave that to your imagination, but it definitely has a glam appeal, and every time you walk in, you will enjoy the experience.

Lines

There is only one line to get into the VIP lounge, and it's usually very short as traffic flows all day in and out.

Cocktails

If I recall correctly, there are at least one or two bars in the lounge, with minimal wait times. I also remember a refreshments table with coffee and water.

Food

There was no food served in the VIP Lounge, but I do recall seeing servers dishing out little appetizers on occasion. (Again, a friendly reminder if you're going to day drink all day: please have a good solid breakfast before you go to BravoCon and plan a midday meal in the Bravo Bazaar). The appetizers served in the VIP lounge are not the size of a restaurant appetizer, just a bit on a spoon. I will add that if Lays sponsors again, you might see a big table of chips. Ha-ha.

Photo Ops

The VIP Lounge offers numerous photo ops throughout the three days of BravoCon. There are many stages for photo ops, some are larger, and some are on the side, some are pop-ups in the middle. It's kind of like a Bravoleb carnival. The setups change frequently; you can leave the VIP Lounge and go back in two hours later, and everything has changed. This is why the VIP lounge is worth that ticket. It's so fun and surprising!

Just like the photo ops in the big tent, all the stages have people taking photos for you with your phone.

Bravolebs

When you aren't expecting it, you will see a Bravoleb in the wild just doing their thing! I arrived one morning early and went right to the bar and saw a fabulously dressed woman at the bar, all by herself. Who was that doll? Lisa Hochstein! I literally was like, "What the heck!" She was in the wild all by herself. That meant I got all the time I wanted with her, and I took full advantage of talking about BravoCon, our Facebook Group, and other fun stuff. She was so playful; she took my crown and put it on. We made some videos and took a lot of pictures. It was like my own little cocktail party. Again, these are the little surprises you will never expect during your three-day experience.

I also found a good spot to just hang out and relax back by the water and refreshments. I also quickly realized this was a good spot to catch Bravolebs walking in the VIP lounge. As soon as

I saw one come in, I nabbed a photo op with them if I could. I didn't see many as I was busy doing VIP Lounge activities, but I spotted Colin from Below Deck coming out from the black curtain. This is just a tip if you're looking for something to do and take a little break!

Then for my big story, I was just scooting around and looked over to the couches and saw Patricia Altschul sitting by herself on a couch. Surrounding her in a circle of chairs were her six security guards. Did that stop me from talking to her? No way. I found that to be an open door for me, or maybe an invite: "You should come talk to me. I'm all alone!" I asked one of the guards if I could say hi to her, and they said they would ask. Being kind and asking gets you much farther than busting in and trying to break the rules. They asked, she said yes, and I walked to the couch and sat next to Patricia for quite a while, actually. Some photos were taken, and I got up. Later on, I did something I probably should not have done, but when you are having the time of your life and whooping it up a bit too much, liquid courage can kick in, and you do something you might be embarrassed by later. Ronnie from Watch What Crappens was sitting next to Patricia, and in my defense, they looked like they weren't in deep conversation at that moment as others were talking to them both, so I asked Ronnie for a quick photo op.

Bad? Yes, but I had no regrets. He was smiling happily in our selfie. I swore to be more thoughtful coming years.

I had a marvelous time in the VIP lounge, and as I said, you could spend all your time there, but it's best to use it as a "Time for the VIP Lounge" stop along the journey of your day. There is so much to experience, and the VIP lounge can be considered just one of the stops of your day. For those not getting a VIP ticket, you can experience many other BravoCon events and buy a Bravopalooza ticket to get a similar experience in a small bite.

Next up is the BravoCon "Extras" that you will experience at BravoCon!

Large Photo-Op Banners Everywhere

Every turn you make at BravoCon, you will be right in front of a large photo banner—this is actually what I love about the BravoCon atmosphere. You always feel you are in the experience. They don't miss a beat with these banners, either with funny, off-the-wall quotes, great backdrops, memes—it's all part of the event. They are literally everywhere, and people take photo ops with these all the time. Find your favorite and take all the pics you want off the wall photos you want. You will not have time to even see them all. I keep finding new ones in the Facebook Group that I have never seen before.

Pop-up Photo Ops

The Bravo Bazaar room hosts the most "activations," which are considered a 2-5 minute interactive event you can participate in with photo ops or a video for yourself. Outside of the Bazaar, there aren't as many, but you can find them outside of the Forum. Outside ones are scenes of Bravo shows and these are always a hit with the members. It seems every year, Bravo sets up a few activations that go viral, and word gets out. Before long, everyone wants to do it. The lines for these can be long, so be ready for that! The best one was in 2019. They had the opening of a Bravo show. You could use props, and they made you a video doing a scene in the show. It was really what I think helped BravoCon take off as an iconic memory for the OGs of the first BravoCon.

There are many others, though, and some are just a quick walk-through. However, there is more to do at BravoCon! They really put in the time and consideration to make this event worth every penny of that ticket.

Bravoland

Bravoland offers a historical view of all your favorite Bravo TV shows set in scenes from the show. You can sit down and use the props and take pictures, or you can just walk and see iconic items from shows. In 2022, I did see Bravoland but didn't take the time to do a full tour, sadly, and in 2023, I didn't do the tour. It's on my list for the upcoming events, though! So, unfortunately, I don't have a lot of stories about my own experience, but there are so many fun photos that members of the BravoCon Facebook Group sent me. I'm making videos of all their pictures and sharing them on my social accounts if you want to follow along. I'll be making them until the next BravoCon, and it's awesome to share all the group's greatest memories.

BravoCon Live Stage

The hottest mini-stage that many of us talked about last year was the BravoCon Live Stage. When you enter the Forum, go down the hallway to the left and the live stage is there at the bottom of the escalators. It might be in a different place in 2024, but my BravoCon Facebook Group will know as soon as the schedule is out. Last year, many of us didn't even know the stage was there. It's not hidden, but you do need to know where it is and the schedule.

The stage sits in front of the escalators. There are spots to stand in front and in the back are stadium seats. If you're disabled, they will escort you to the area where you can sit on closer chairs and put your scooters to the left of the crowd, closer to the front.

You should put it on your tour of the day. Just like everything else at Bravo, every hour changes, so be sure to make time when you arrive that morning to find out what's on the schedule.

These live stage shows can be described as live interviews to a game show style theme or a fun quiz to, well, anything! There's lots of laughs and cheers. I'd like to say almost a pop-up panel of sorts. And I say that because I don't recall seeing these on the mobile app unless I'm wrong, and I might be!

These seemed to run all day all 3-days of the event, so take time to find the schedule and put it in your day! You can also see these on Peacock after BravoCon!

BravoCon After Dark

Every year, Bravo hosts a BravoCon After Dark party at another venue other than the Forum. In 2023, it was hosted at Caesar's Palace outdoor terrace and balcony level of OMNIA. These are higher-priced tickets that you can purchase closer to the event. They have a special guest star, and last year, DJ Steve Aoki took the stage. In 2022, James Kennedy was the star of the night DJ'ing, and in 2019, Tom Sandoval and his band played.

This event is a party on its own, so if you're planning on going, prepare to have the energy to go. BravoCon on day two can be exhausting itself, so I highly recommend that you take a break after BravoCon, relax and maybe even nap if you can. Eat a good dinner and then head out later to the After Dark party. My regret last year was that I did back-to-back events on Saturday after BravoCon that I was too tired to attend that night. I still might consider going again, but I learned my life balance needs. I'm also older, and my energy was low, but if you really want to attend, have that nightclub energy! From the pictures and stories, everyone had a great time and Bravolebs showed up and danced and engaged with the Bravoholics!

Info from 2023

- BravoCon After Dark is Saturday, November 4th, starting at 9 pm at OMNIA Nightclub inside Caesars Palace Las Vegas Hotel & Casino.
- The party will take place on the balcony level of the club and

outdoor terrace with guest DJ entertainment and Bravolebs in attendance. You won't want to miss it! Until 10:30 pm, the club belongs to Bravo! After, the party continues when the main level of the club opens to the public, where Steve Aoki will perform late night. The balcony and terrace will remain private just for us until close! All included with your ticket. Your ticket includes light bites and a $100 pre-loaded bar card upon entry.

- Limited tickets are available, so grab them before they're gone TODAY, starting at 12 pm ET/9 am PT, while supplies last.
- Tickets to this exclusive event are $449 plus taxes and fees for a full night of fun.
- Please keep in mind that the OMNIA Nightclub dress code is strictly enforced and can prohibit entry if not followed. Upscale dress is recommended. No pool attire, such as t-shirts, tanks, or flip-flops, is allowed.

CHAPTER 13

TICKETS! TICKETS! TICKETS!

B's, this chapter is one of the reasons I decided to write this book. Since 2019, for the past 3 BravoCon's, I have helped members with buying and selling tickets. Each year, some things change, but Bravo now has a pretty standard process for selling. What has changed, though, is the number of people wanting to go, fewer tickets on sale, people wishing to sell their tickets, and, unfortunately, scammers catching on and ruining the joy for so many others last year. The number of people who messaged me to verify tickets was overwhelming. The number of people who want to sell tickets was more than in 2022. It was a wild ride for myself and Suzy! Sharri is also one of our moderators, and she helped, too. I also asked 3 other gals— Jamie, Kim, and Angi—to help moderate during BravoCon, and we ended up bringing them on early to help moderate, as the group was on fire with everything going on at once! Tickets, posts, new members, woo hoo!

Now that I've had a lot of time to learn everything from last year, I have created a better process for buying and selling in our group, and it won't require much help from the moderators, who, by the way, don't get paid. Suzy and I don't get paid either! We all do this stuff for the love of Bravo and our members!

Bravo TV will announce to the general public when tickets go on sale. As I have already mentioned, it's typically 3 months before the event, but my Meghan King Edmonds PI skills are sharp, and I'm guessing that the tickets might be out sooner this time around, but who knows! From what I have read online, big conventions tend to sell tickets many months before the event, and BravoCon is now a big event. Fingers crossed!

Things to Prepare for:

- Join our Facebook Group! https://www.Facebook.com/groups/BravoCon
- Verify your credit card has enough on it for a big purchase (you never know!)
- Verify your address is correct.
- Double-check your 3-digit pin, zip code, and other details; ensure everything is accurate.
- Know what tickets you want to buy.

BravoCon Pre-Sale

It's no secret that we have been gifted pre-sale tickets in the past; everyone knows about it, and I wrote about it in this book. I cannot guarantee that Bravo will offer us that early bird promotion again, but let's all cross our fingers!!! We are not the only group or content creator that gets the pre-sale, so there are a lot of Bravoholics rushing that day!

Pre-Sale is usually at 12:00 EST, and you had better be ready. Don't confuse your time zones if you live in California; that's 9:00 for you.

Have Many Devices Ready!

From reading what the members said over the years, they prepare with many devices: phones, iPads, computers, and laptops. Some even give their friends or husbands the links. It's really a "whoever gets it first" game here.

Link to Buy

Test the link to buy the day it's announced; be sure you can see the page. It will say something about a countdown or not being available yet. If you can't see the page, try other browsers.

When Tickets are On Sale

Some said last year that tickets went on sale early, some said late. Either way, everyone started refreshing, and if they got lucky and could get the link to buy open, they had to buy fast. Do not over think this buying process! If you wait, your selected tickets might not hold, and if your link gets wonky due to whatever reason, some people said they had to start over and got the "sold out" message on the website. Website glitches are to be expected for a few reasons, most likely because the site is overloaded with requests.

Don't fret, B's. The most typed words in the group last year were "Keep trying!!!" Many people got the "sold out" page the entire time but kept checking and eventually got a ticket to pop up. And this went on all day, by the way, my B's! We had people posting at 5:00 in the afternoon, saying they tried and got some. I think this might be due to those glitches I mentioned. If the site is overloaded, it might be miscalculating the tickets available, then has time to propagate the correct amount and more are released.

Next Day/Official Sales Day

If you missed tickets on pre-sale day, then you have a shot at it again the next day. They will release more. These tickets are for those in the general public who didn't get a notice through the regular Bravo TV broadcast of messages (texts, emails, social media).

Nothing changes on the official sale day; rinse and repeat the last few bullet points above.

Take note: There is a wait list that Bravo will have if you get the SOLD-OUT page. At least they had it last year, and it worked for some, so sign up!

Sold Out

Well, eventually, they are officially sold out, typically on sales day. If you got tickets, congratulations! If you didn't, there is still hope! There are many legitimate ways to buy tickets!

Bravo Official Wait List

The members talked about the wait list, and some felt defeated that it would never open up, but many did get the wait list tickets. Just hold on to hope. There is no one to contact that I know of. Just wait it out. The ticket agency is ok to work with, but they will most likely not have information. And from what I recall members saying, they did ask and didn't get any answers. No one really knows; it's just a waitlist.

Buying Off-Site StubHub, etc.

The most popular question in the Facebook Group was, "Should I buy my ticket off StubHub?" The answer is you should decide that yourself. StubHub is going to tack on a large upsell fee and it's a lot. They know how in-demand these tickets are, so you could pay double or more for any ticket! I know of a couple that paid a very high amount off StubHub because they wanted to go that bad. Be prepared for this, and trust me, it will get higher the closer we get to the event. Last-minute FOMO is going to be expensive. There are going to be other sites selling these tickets, too. Watch out for them, and be sure they are legitimate. You can ask the group this question if you're wondering! Every year, things change.

Buying and Selling on Our BravoCon Facebook Group

First up will be digital ticket sales, then wristbands after they arrive. These happen in two different sales timelines. Usually, we hold ticket sales until September or so, but last year, due to demand and people wanting to sell due to their own need to cancel (sadly!), we allowed ticket sales earlier, mid-August or so. Then, when the wristbands arrived, we had more people who needed to sell, and things picked up even more. Our group hosted so many ticket sales from August to the time of the event. Many were 3-day VIP and 1-day VIP tickets. In fact, everything was coming through our queue.

How I Plan On Allowing Ticket Sales Next Year

Suzy and I will decide when we will open up ticket sales. That day, we will have formal rules posted and pinned in our featured discussions. We are usually pretty firm that everyone follows the rules. Some folks will have special accommodation, of course, but following the guides is helpful.

Pricing Your Tickets

In our group, you can only sell tickets for the price you paid. Every Bravoholic buys a ticket with the intention of going and will only cancel if something comes up, so we know how important these tickets are. No one "gets to make a buck" in our group. If you try to sneak in a ticket sale for profit, the group will report you or tag us—I guarantee it. Follow the rules, or you will be blocked. We have had a few people say, "Well if I can make money, I want to." Sad, but no. Not in our group!

Selling

If you want to sell your tickets, you will need to post a picture of the ticket with your name and address on it in the group. This post will not be live in the group; it will be in our "New posts" moderation queue. Suzy and the mod team will not be approving those posts, only myself. If it passes my sniff test, then I will message you to move to the next level. Please watch for your filtered message requests! Then, you and I will have a quick video call to have you show me your digital/printed receipt and verify you are a real person. Videos sent to me will not be accepted because scammers have learned that trick. I also will take time to review your Facebook profile and verify you are a real person. This is something all the mods did last year; we were all non-paid ticket angels.

After you pass my test (it should be quick, not a long process), then I will reach out to my Patreon "Wait list" group (my paid subscribers here on Patreon are first in line). They will be offered the chance to buy the tickets. They then need to go through their own verification process. I'm the first verifier, and I'm pretty good at it, but again, it's at your discretion to buy with someone you feel comfortable with. This process might seem a bit longer, but selling a ticket isn't urgent. There are plenty of buyers waiting. When you decide to sell a ticket, think of it as selling a car or a house. Quick ticket sales are like going to a cheap car sales lot.

Ticket Buyers

I will have a shared Google doc with a number dedicated to you based on your membership number when you joined my Patreon. No names will be listed but at least you can check it and find out how close you are to getting tickets. I needed to figure out an easy way to organize this, and that will work as it's open for everyone to check.

What if you're not on a Patreon subscriber list and want to get on my waitlist?

This is for people who bought my book after Black Friday, November 2024. You can still subscribe to my Patreon as a newsletter or paid subscriber. I will give you a number, add you to my Google doc, and send you a link.

Payments

We only recommend buying and selling through PayPal or Venmo. These were the most popular as they had protection. I'm not an expert in this area, but all the scammers were using Zelle as it's easy to get through them. Normal people don't "take credit cards." PayPal and Venmo are most common, but again, verify!

Scammers

Things went pretty well last year, initially, until the scam group launched, and people searching for "BravoCon" found them and our awesome group. That scam group quickly grew, and that's when all the issues started. I will go into the scammers in the next section, but this is super important. Know everything you can before you get sold a bad wristband or digital ticket.

We do not allow ticket sales in posts, comments, or community chats. You might see people trying to sell their "fake tickets" to others, saying they are looking or whatever. Not only is our group protective, but they also report these comments. Our group, the mod team, Suzy and I, care so much about each other that we all protect each other. It's actually quite amazing to see such a strong bond, strangers helping strangers. You will see it next year, I guarantee it. And not just with ticket sales but with questions, help, tips, etc.

"Other Facebook Groups"

I use quotes because I found none last year that were legitimate. This is your warning for next year. You might be tempted to look around. These groups are all run by scammers who have scammers as administrators. They learned our language last year, they learned what we did in our group, they had scammers in our group, they knew the right keywords to say, and they knew how to get in your head. They knew how to reach out to your private messenger and knew how to negotiate a good VIP deal. Do not fall for this, and please do not come to our group and post the question, "Am I getting scammed?" because those posts will not be allowed next year. Also, our moderators and I have the group so well trained. We are not going to chat with members who ask us that. If anyone is asking us that, it means they are not paying attention to what group they are in (not ours) and are not reading our posts. If you know me, you'll know I post about scammers and warnings all the time.

Wristbands

These are usually sent out a month before the event. Watch the Facebook Group; you will see posts of people posting their wristbands with excitement! We love seeing this!!! But I'm going to warn you all now: Due to the number of people that come into our group from ticket sales day to the event, we can't control the new members as easily as we can now during our off-season. I recommend you put something on your picture if you want to post it, like a watermark of sorts, so if the image does get stolen and used in other groups, others will know it's a scammer stealing it. We do a good job of vetting legitimate members, but the scammers are quick!

Once you receive your wristband, as tempted as you are to put it on, do not do this. They are very hard to take off, and we have had members who had to call in and get replacements to pick up at will call due to this. Some could get them off, but many did not. Members found YouTube videos that showed some hacks on how to get them off.

Will Call

There is a will call booth when you first enter BravoCon, before the official entrance area. Many people will be in line for this, so if you need "will call," get in line early if you want to experience more time at BravoCon. I had to get will call last year, and I had to wait in line for a bit. It was worth it but outside BravoCon is a carnival in itself! Everyone is happy no matter what, in line or not in line!

To Close

Last year, all the mods, Suzy, and I donated a lot of volunteer hours with the ticket sales, and while we all loved helping, I told them all that I was going to change this and not ask them to help because this is a non-paid volunteer passion hobby. That's why I wrote the book, got subscribers, and I want to earn some money helping. Our group is private and not on the public internet. I want to earn some money finally, and I'll work my tail off for it, as well. I want to protect and serve our group. We are a loyal bunch and everyone in the group knows my loyalty level is beyond 100%. So, finally, in year five, I'm making content to sell and selling my time to help you all have a better experience and a way to earn. I want to keep promotions and sponsors out of the group. No one likes "Sponsored ads" like you see on Instagram or TikTok. I'd rather have a silent role in that and keep the group fun and always energetic!

CHAPTER 14

THE BRAVOCON CHECKLIST AND TRAVEL TIPS

You might be reading this when you're not at the time of ticket purchasing yet. I am going to write it, though, as you are completely done with the exciting wild ride of securing all of your tickets. There is a path to successfully attending BravoCon, and the tickets are a 2–3-month online adventure on its own!

You can finally have a sense of "quiet and safety" once you have your wristband in your hands. It's like a reward for all your hard work from the time tickets were announced until you bought the last batch of digital tickets you needed to buy. Now you can get to planning the fun stuff! Easy low-stress planning.

The rest of the time, I love filling my schedule with little things like planning what to bring, what to wear, goals to meet Bravolebs, and organizing meetups and surprises! I'll be sure not to spill the beans in the next few chapters about the experience itself, but I'll give you a run-down of things you might want to know that none of us knew back in 2023 when we did BravoCon Vegas for the first time. There is a lot to know, but I feel confident to let you know all the important things, so you can relax a bit. Also remember that since you bought this book, you could ask our community on Facebook any questions.

The Checklist

For some, your checklist might need an Excel spreadsheet, a Word document, or some type of task planner. For me, I keep a notepad on my computer of all my notes for everything and then before I fly out, I print the list and keep an electronic copy on my phone and in email. I don't keep the list I print in my purse but on my person because of "what ifs" like losing my purse, theft, a lost phone, etc. I fly alone and go alone, so I always think of my own safety. Thinking about these events, I might just get a little wallet to put in my bra or my pants. I might be a worry wart, but I'll be prepared.

My checklist includes:

- Flight Info
- Hotel information
- Printed BravoCon digital ticket QR codes
- Phone numbers for Vegas locations I might need to call (Forum main number, my hotel front desk number)
- Phone numbers of other people I know going (in case I lose my phone)

- Phone numbers of important people I need to call back home in case something bad happens
- Insurance information (health, car, etc.)
- Credit card information
- Cash
- Anything else I can think of

Travel into Vegas

Many members in the Facebook Group fly in on Wednesday to get a head start. I am one of those people! I like to get in later in the afternoon and spend all Wednesday meeting up with the other members flying in, getting our rooms all figured out, and just having fun doing what I want. I don't take vacations often, so I try to make sure I make the most of this trip. Thursday for me is a big day as I have to prepare for the big meetup on Thursday nights. I like to lounge around Thursday morning and get my hair done Thursday afternoon, meet up for drinks, hang out, and watch other members start to get into the hotel. For me, this is just as exciting as seeing the Bravolebs. I adore seeing the members all excited, saying hello, and sharing stories.

If you're not like me and want to fly in on Thursday, this seems like the time everyone tends to fly in. It gives you enough time to get settled in for the big weekend and get ready for Friday.

If you want to fly in on Friday, due to having Saturday and Sunday tickets, there are plenty of things going on with the Bravoverse on Friday so just get settled in the hotel and head to the Forum! Everyone is outside the Forum all day during BravoCon, and you don't need a ticket to hang out with others. You could use my tips on meeting Bravolebs in Chapter 18.

Fly in on Saturday? Some did that, too! Everyone does what they want. I know a gal in 2022 in NYC who flew in early Sunday morning and flew home the same day. She was die-hard for a one day experience and got it!

Flying Home

In 2022, I was living in Fort Myers, FL, and booked all my flights and hotel before I knew there was going to be a Cat 5 Hurricane I'd have to survive. Two weeks prior to BravoCon, my life was in an uproar of disaster, power issues, and internet problems. It was a heavy time for me. My life was completely upside down, but I was still so happy I had BravoCon to escape to and forget everything for a few days. I flew in on Wednesday, and that was still a great idea as I had more time to prepare for the meetup and all the things I had planned. Remember this is me and my life and managing the BravoCon Facebook Group. I feel I'm of service to the group, and while I am not owed anything, I always like to be at events early and stay late. I had booked my flight home on Monday, and while it was fine, I felt that for 2023, I should stay an extra day to get more relaxing time in, as BravoCon is a 72-hour whirlwind of a time.

2023 was a bit different. When I was booking my flights, I decided to stay that extra day. I flew in on Wednesday because that was what I wanted to do, but I had issues finding decent flights home. In 2023, I moved back home to a small town in Minnesota with limited flight options. My travel arrangements were complicated: I had to take an Uber to a hotel in my town, then a bus to Minneapolis, and finally, a direct flight to Vegas (thank goodness). Being disabled, I had my rollator with me and needed to arrange for handicapped assistance. It was a lot to figure out, but nothing was stopping me!

I booked my hotels from Wednesday through Tuesday morning. I had my flights and travel all figured out. Then, on Saturday, I changed my mind. I was looking at my itinerary and saw that my return trip would get me home at 3:00 AM on Wednesday. Good grief, what was I thinking when I booked that flight? I think I was so excited I forgot the hours of travel drama. I knew after Sunday, the third day of BravoCon, I wouldn't really have much to do. So, on Monday, I needed to relax there. I really would rather relax on my couch. I found a ticket home on Monday that was a bit better, bought it, and lost the money I paid on the original return flight. I wanted to be in my own bed by Monday night. And it happened! I enjoyed Sunday at BravoCon with all its glory, knowing that I didn't have that regrettable trip home.

Lesson learned? Always buy changeable or refundable tickets. It was a costly decision. Vegas can change a person, and for me, that was it. Maybe I'll meet Mr. Bravo, and I'll want to stay an extra day and hang out—you never know! But I'll be ready with my changeable tickets in hand!

Most people fly in on Thursday and leave on Monday. That's what I have heard members say the most. Keep in mind that our big meetup is on Thursday nights, so if you want to make it, fly in mid-afternoon so you can get ready and join us for the big kick-off party!

CHAPTER 15

TRANSPORTATION, HOTELS, FOOD, DISABLED ACCESS, LUGGAGE

This chapter is about the little things to think about for your trip. If you are an experienced traveler or convention goer, you are probably all set with your trip plans. For those who are new to Vegas or a convention, this chapter should be helpful.

I'm also going to be writing in my "I went to BravoCon solo" mode in the next chapter. Even though I manage the BravoCon Facebook Group, I still went to Vegas by myself, did everything by myself, and met up with people once I got there. So, if you are in the same position, the tips in my next chapter might come in handy for you. If I did it, you can too!

I also know the majority of you reading this have no issues walking or getting around. However, I decided to write additional notes for those who are disabled or who have walking challenges.

Transportation

Unless you want first-class transportation, you're like the majority of us who get a taxi or cab at the airport or go to the Uber/Lyft area. I found out prior to coming to Vegas that the Uber/Lyft area is a bit of a walk to get to from the arrival terminal. I did not want to deal with that as I use a rollator, so I opted to get a taxi cab which is right outside of the arrival terminal. I also found out from my taxi driver that getting a taxi in Vegas is a fixed rate (in 2023, it was $30) for a ride to the hotel, and he said this was the basic price all taxi cab drivers have to charge as they are under different rules and laws. Lyft and Uber can have different prices, and due to traffic and busy times, you might pay more. I don't really know, but I thought I'd share this tip from my taxi cab driver.

Using the taxi service also dropped me off right at the LINQ hotel entrance, which was very convenient for me with my walking challenges. The Uber/Lyft drop-off was down the driveway quite a bit, and with all my luggage and my rollator, it would have been more of a walk than I was expecting. The taxi cab area is also where I saw Caroline Stanbury from Housewives of Dubai. I wish my phone took better pictures; she was gorgeous!!

Hotels

In 2023, Bravo sent out hotel links for the event so those attending could get in on a large group room rate. For the upcoming events, Bravo has already sent out their booked room links. More than likely, these will have all been reserved by the time you're reading this. The three hotels they had booked group rates for were LINQ, Harrah's, and Caesars. All three are very close to the Forum and easy to get to by walking.

Many people who are Vegas lovers know their favorite hotels and know how to get around with the monorail, Ubers, taxis, etc. Not everyone stays at the LINQ, Harrah's, and Caesars. I read the comments of the Facebook members, and many stay at other hotels on and off-strip.

Remember back in my budget chapter? This will be important when booking your hotel. Some of the off-strip hotels will be cheaper, but you might need to find transportation to get to the Forum. The strip hotels will be much more expensive, and you will still need to figure out transportation or walk. Walking is what I read most people do as the strip is enjoyable to walk with all the people and attractions. If you want to be close, then book a hotel close to the Forum.

The hotels are just like any other hotel. They come with extra fees, taxes, surcharges, and, well, unexpected charges that you might not know about. If you're concerned, be sure to call the hotel and find out when you have booked your hotel. Also, ask about the cancellation policy, and if you need a handicapped room or any special requests, make sure to add that to your booking.

As I am handicapped and rented a mobility scooter, I made sure to let them know, and they booked me a room that had room for my mobility scooter. It was more like a small living room, but I moved the coffee table out of the way for my scooter. I did not get any upgrades for this; that's just how that room was.

I verified my room reservation a few weeks before I flew to Vegas for peace of mind that I was all set.

Vegas hotel check-ins are not like your small hotel in a normal city. They do have a check-in area if you want to talk to a real person, but they have check-in terminals for quicker check-in. This was all new to me, and it didn't take long to figure it out. The keys came out of an ATM-type machine. The check-in was right around the corner when you walked into the LINQ from the taxi cab stands.

And if you need bell service, then you go to the bell desk. It was very close to the check-in terminals. Everything was pretty smooth when I arrived, to be honest.

Food

The LINQ has 30 or so restaurants, little snack shops, and just about everything you need at the hotel. I found a liquor store, little pharmacies, a tattoo parlor, and, yep, pizza in a vending machine right by the elevator. (I got one, and it wasn't bad). I guess all the big hotels will have everything you need when you stay there, so food will not be hard to find if you don't want to venture outside of your hotel during BravoCon. Many members in the group talked about other dining plans and where they went, and some were like me; I got food at the hotel and outside of the hotel. I didn't order room service as it was only by Door Dash and decided it wasn't for me.

Remember how I mentioned you might forget about food during BravoCon? It's a real thing, especially during the event.

So, fueling up before you go to the event is super important. There is food at BravoCon, but you are having so much fun that food isn't a top priority.

I didn't fuel up big, though, every morning. I typically got a coffee and muffin from the café by the elevator. I also got Dunkin donuts, so it was not the healthiest, but I wasn't hungry most of the day, either. It's up to you and what you require. There are food options in the Bravo Bazaar area.

When I was doing final planning for my agenda for the trip in 2023, I knew I had a lot of holes for dinner options at night. Honestly, I didn't do much night-evening dining out. Many times, I just stopped at this other café in the LINQ that had many food choices; it was delicious and just filling enough. I ate alone in my room. So I could relax and wind down. Leave yourself some room for this downtime in case you need it. You can always add on big night-outs as plans happen. Basically, leave room for unexpected surprises or rest time. You might end up meeting new friends during the day, and your whole night can be a completely different plan than what you thought.

Disabled Access

I had a fear of traveling to big events when I became more disabled and had walking issues. In 2017, I was walking fine and didn't need any assistance. I was living in Vegas at the time and had to travel to Minneapolis for a couple of days, and then I was off to Chicago to present at a convention. On the trip to Minneapolis, I found my arthritic knee was not happy, and I could not walk once I got to the hotel. I was very scared, mostly about what I was going to do when I got to Chicago. I almost canceled my trip and was so upset about everything. Then, I learned about mobility scooters and found a company that rented them in Chicago. I got one dropped off at my hotel, and I spent the next few days using that to get around the hotel and other places I had to go. Once I learned about this, my travel got a bit easier to navigate. When the 2019 BravoCon was announced, I was again hit with fear as I didn't know how to manage the locations and how I would get around. My arthritis was worse, and it just wasn't something I was interested in, so sadly, I missed the 2019 BravoCon.

In 2022, I was not going to miss BravoCon for anything! I prepared all my disability lists and learned everything I needed to prior to the event. I found out Javits rented scooters onsite, and for the walking I had to do, I could use my rollator. NYC was great for Ubers, and I didn't have to walk too far without the rollator. It was a win for me, and I had a great trip!

In 2023, I knew Vegas was ready for me and it is a town built for everyone of all ages and disabilities. I found many online mobility scooter rental companies and found one that seemed reputable and put in an online reservation. I selected Scootaround. I called their 800 number and found their customer service excellent.

I booked the scooter for a drop-off at my hotel. Due to their policy, they could only drop it off in the Uber/Lyft area. The driver called me to verify the drop-off. I asked him to come to the taxi cab area, and he did. I told him I had a rollator and was alone, so it would be more challenging for me. What a great guy. He dropped it off, and I was so happy.

If you are new to a scooter, be sure to practice driving it around to learn the speeds and brakes, but it's super easy and fun! I got around very fast. The only big issue I had in the hotel room was getting into the room by myself. I figured out a way to lean into the scooter handlebars, and I could put in my key and then push the power handle and push the door open with my scooter. It wasn't easy, but it got easier. I could drive it into the room and park it in the little living room area I had. Backing out was not bad either, I opened the door with my hand and then held it open and scooted out. I hope next year I get the same type of room, as it was perfect.

Once I got out of the room, the scooter was easy to get around everywhere in Vegas, with the exception of one restaurant in the LINQ. I would not recommend going there if you have a scooter. You can message me if you want to know which restaurant I am referring to. I don't want to shame them, but it was very challenging, and I wish I had gone to another restaurant.

During BravoCon, the Forum is 100% ready for scooters! I had zero issues getting around. The hallways were so large that there was room for many people. The Bravo Live Stage had an area for people in mobility scooters too. The staff see you on the scooter and always try to make you feel accommodated and offer special help to get in line or get through lines easier. You do not need to even worry about "what people think" or "what people will think."

Who might want a mobility scooter? Anyone with walking issues, standing issues, foot/leg injuries, back problems, or any issues with being on your feet all day long. There are a lot of places to sit, but if you need to stand in line for a while and are not comfortable, then you will want a scooter so you can sit and wait in line. The lines at BravoCon in 2023 were not as long as they were in 2022, but you are going to be doing a lot of walking either way. Members talked about putting on 20,000 steps, mostly because you are busy all day doing this and doing that, walking from room to room down long hallways, and then going outside to the photo ops and, well, generally being a busy Bravo fan! There is so much to do!

I remember reading a story of a gal who got injured right before BravoCon, and she got a scooter and made it such a fun story. She took all these special, fun pics in her scooter, and I was so jealous. I wish I had thought of that!

Outside of the scooter access, I didn't notice any other issues for myself, being a person who's physically disabled and also a person of size. I didn't have issues finding regular seating/bathrooms, etc. I didn't need any special accommodations. If you have other disabilities and require special accommodations or have specific questions, please reach out to me, and I can talk to Bravo and find out for you. Bravo will always take care of its fans at events who need anything to make their experience the same as everyone else. Security has their eye on people who need special care; they went out of their way to make sure I was taken care of.

Extra Luggage

Ok ok, not really a topic you thought you'd need to read, but here we are. I was one of those people who:

- Overpacked
- Forgot to wear my cutest shirt on Sunday and ended up wearing a crappy outfit and looked like crap!
- Needed to ship stuff home!

If you are going to buy extra merch from the Bravo Bazaar, be sure you have room to take it home. Thinking back to Sunday, day three, and seeing my bed full of "Bravo stash" and extra stuff, I knew I needed more luggage next time.

I think bulkier items, like hoodies, shirts, and stuff, are what will get you. Most people who buy merch from the Bravolebs buy smaller items. Just ensure you leave some room for the purchases when you are packing because there will be some no doubt!

CHAPTER 16

TIPS FOR SOLOS & BRAVOCON ON A BUDGET

Who wants to go on a 3-day big weekend alone? I do! I read a lot of comments last year and in 2022 prior to BravoCon about members in our group being worried about going alone; many also had budget concerns. To help you folks, I combined the two topics for this chapter and will fill you in on every tip I have. I went alone in 2022 and 2023, and I am happy to share my own experience.

Solos

I have been to a few conventions outside of my area and went alone. I am one of those people who enjoys travel and going alone is not a concern. I know some of you might have worries about safety or what you will do without someone to talk to. Let me ease your mind a bit about BravoCon. I went alone both in 2022 and 2023. Sure, I had other people in the group to meet up with, but I spent a lot of time alone at the event, doing my own thing and soaking up every bit of the experience. I did not travel to Vegas with anyone. I got to my hotel just fine and settled in my room alone. Even though I had Suzy, my partner, to meet up with, we did not go out together every day. I went to the Forum on my own, and Suzy did too. I think the "alone" feeling just goes away when you're at an event of this size. The energy is so high, and everyone is so happy that it's hard to think, "I'm alone."

As you walk around, you'll notice that so many people are alone. I will admit it's nice to have people to meet up with and catch an event with, but in the end, Suzy and I split up often to go do our own thing. I'll offer you some tips to find your own "Suzy" in the BravoCon Facebook Group or just go it alone! At the end of this chapter, there are a few members of the group who offer a tip for the solos! (these are some of our top contributors who are also very helpful and friendly).

If you want to be a part of the biggest BravoCon family online, our group is just that! We have our own Bravoverse going on, and for some, the group is their "go-to" because we discuss everything Bravo, even between BravoCon seasons. If you want to make new friends, this is the group to do that! If you want to just lurk and read, that's just fine too. There is no rule about contributing. Just enjoy the group is all we ask. Below is a list of things I thought of for Vegas:

- Join the BravoCon Facebook Group!
- After you join, check out all of our featured discussions

(posts) at the top of the page and read our rules. We are a well-managed group and are 100% full of Bravoholics!

- In time, we will create a Chat in the group for "Solos," and that chat will have members talking about creating their own meetups and just getting to know each other. Many small groups have been created, and solos going alone have their "Suzy" to meet up with or have dinner with, etc. Right now, our 2023 Solos Chat has 1026 members in it. That group might continue.

- Feel free to create your own post if you're looking to meet up with some of the members. It's sometimes easier to have new friends who are in the same hotel and doing a similar panel/event that you are interested in. These types of posts are more common when people are looking to share photo ops with others or meet up for something at BravoCon. Some just want to meet for breakfast, too!

Other Tips at BravoCon

If you're alone and want to meet people, look for others who are alone and spark up a Bravo discussion. This is definitely not hard to do! When you're in line is your best bet; the lines take a while to get through, and if you find someone else alone, they might want to talk. One topic that's an easy icebreaker is "Are you in the BravoCon Facebook Group?" Because so many members are, that topic is enough. I know because members told me this, and it gave me so much joy to know the group was something so many had in common! You could also just ask them, "What's your favorite thing you have seen?" or "Have you met any Bravolebs yet?" These are simple, easy topics that everyone should want to discuss. You can also sit by other solos at the panels, BravoCon live stage, sitting outside (many benches full of people back by the photo ops), and the Bravo Bazaar too! If someone is not interested in chatting, like normal life, we all get the hint. But this event is usually high energy, and everyone is so happy. We all love talking about Bravo.

How do I know these tips work? Because I used all of these tips myself. Sometimes, I found myself in a long line and just sparked up conversations with someone standing by me. It's so fun and so easy. That's why going solo is so great, too!

Tips From Our Members

Amanda Foust: "Do not be afraid of going solo! You will never feel alone since you are surrounded by people with the same interests but will still have freedom."

Shannon Stern: "Going solo this year was great! I met so many new friends that I knew from this group, went to the same events throughout the day/weekend with, stayed at the same hotel with, flew into town with, etc. The best part about going solo? You trade phone numbers and can go off and do your own thing when you want to and then rejoin your newfound "crew" when you have the time."

Andrea Spleth Connors : "I was solo this year and had an amazing time. I connected with a few Bravocon FB group members ahead of time and met up with them several times. I never felt alone because I met people and had conversations with so many fun fellow Bravoholics."

Katie Wilson: "Going solo was amazing! I got to go to the panels I wanted and waited in lines for people I wanted to see without asking a friend if that's what they wanted to do. I did what I wanted when I wanted, saw who I wanted, and ate when and where I wanted. It was amazing!"

Desra Manning: "This year was my very first BravoCon to attend. I attended solo and actually loved it! I met SO many amazing ladies that I didn't 'feel alone.' We chatted in BravoPalooza and enjoyed the atmosphere. Comfortable shoes are a MUST. I wore jeans and a blazer. I also took a crossbody purse. Looking back, I would purchase a tote bag first thing and any BravoCon merchandise to ensure sizing is available. (I didn't this time b/c I didn't want to haul it all around until the end of the day) I also attended GA Friday. Next year, I want to attend for 3 days. I would also recommend getting all your water, vitamins, antioxidants in rest, etc., before you go if possible. Maybe take a small backpack too. I would also like to attend an evening event that Andy held—the awards. I watched it on TV, and it looked amazing! Also, I thought cash would be primary, but Caesar's only accepted cards. I purchased the infamous "chicken tenders" and bottled water. I would also suggest walking around the Bravolebs booth, where they sell their merch. You will see so many! I had an absolutely amazing time!!!!"

Kevin Bradley: "I went solo twice (2022 and 2023), and it was the best decision I've ever made! I was hesitant when I went in 2022. But that all went away once I started meeting and hanging out with new people during the weekend. And in 2023, I met up with those same people again and it reminded me that going solo was great. My advice is if you really want to go to Bravocon, do not hesitate to go solo. That should never hold anyone back. It'll be the best thing for you in the end. You'll be surrounded by other solo goers who share a similar interest as you. You will meet new people all weekend, and you can bs about anything related to Bravo. The VIP lounge this year was a big help for solo goers as I saw people who came solo interacting and hanging out with each other all weekend long. That's one of the best things about Bravocon. Should there be a Bravocon 2024, you can bet I'll be going solo again!"

Donna Contos: "Went solo the first time. While it was great, I did feel lonely. It would have been nice to have someone to share the excitement with, etc. I will be attending solo again next year and really hope I will be able to connect with the people in the Solo FB Group to actually meet up for some events. Definitely dress comfortably. Carry a tote or backpack!"

Lindsey Clark: "I'm all for going solo. Not just for BravoCon but for life. Why wait to have a friend who is willing to go with you on any trip? You never know what will happen in life, and if you're ever going to be able to go again, why miss out on the opportunity? I went solo in 2022 and have no regrets. I got to get every photo op I wanted and go to whatever panels and events I wanted to. I wasn't worried about compromising like I would have been if I had gone with someone else. I also got in a group chat with other solo attendees, and we still talk to this day. I hung out with them during Bravocon 2022. I wasn't able to go in 2023, but I was talking to those that did and others that didn't the entire time. We are all already excited to hopefully go next year. I have no regrets."

BravoCon on a Budget

I won't be getting deep on this subject but rather offer a few tips I recall from the members last year. This can also apply to those who didn't get full 3-day tickets and could only buy a 1-day ticket. I know a savvy Bravoholic will make it work!

One-day ticket purchasers can have just as much fun as anyone else! If this is what you can do with your budget, then let's make it count! For starters, if you're still flying to Vegas for all 3 days, then you need to find other activities to do on the days you are not at the event. Figure out your budget and then go find the other activities.

- Post a question in the group! If you're looking for outside the Forum activities, ask the members what else they are doing. You'd be surprised with all the answers you will get; people love sharing all their tips!

- Many members in the group should be licensed FBI agents as they can find anything, and they will post any and all BravoCon information. So, watch the group for this, or feel free to ask if you're looking! Many members have great ideas to help here. I'm busy running the group and stuff, so I leave that fun job for the members to help with.

- Many Bravolebs will host their own shows or events in Vegas during these few days. Many of these shows are under $100, and some include dinner or cocktails. I know that Heather McDonald, Captain Lee, Erika Jayne, Amy Phillips, and probably more had a show. Our group did a group meetup at one of the shows. There will be new options, I'm sure.

- Skip add-ons. If you're really looking to save money, skipping some add-ons can help save you some money. Here is the list of extras for you to consider: Bravopalooza, Bravos, WWHL, After Dark Party

- Hotel hangout. It's a thing, and if you are into this, you can meet a few Bravolebs and have fun going from hotel to hotel. As our group members start to check into hotels, the pictures will start being posted, and then we all figure out what Bravoleb is staying where. I don't recommend you hang out at one hotel to meet a Bravoleb, but a few members mentioned they hung out at night at the casinos and bars to meet their favorites. I'm guessing if a Bravoleb is out in the wild, they most likely want to talk to us, their super fans! I don't recall hearing any horrible stories from any members of a Bravoleb meeting.

- Outside the Forum. While Bravolebs usually don't hang out long outside the Forum, you might get a peek and a quick snap of some of them. Not all Bravolebs are under the heavy security. Some are just out and about like you and enjoy being noticed!

I'm sure Bravo wants everyone to come no matter what and they also play many of the panels and WWHL shows on Peacock after BravoCon if you want to watch again. I believe they did some shows on regular Bravo TV as well.

CHAPTER 17

THE FORUM

BravoCon is such an amazing event. I just had to add information about the venue. You are going to spend a lot of time there, so get to know it a bit! I had to add this for the new people coming, as they will have so many questions. Last year, we all did our searching on Google Maps to figure it out and, of course, we scoped the Caesars website to try to figure the Forum out. I didn't help us one bit. Once you arrive, it's so much different than your mind imagined. Everything you looked up just doesn't matter anymore. With that said, I will not ruin your experience by any means, but maybe offer a bit of a "comfortable" feeling so when you arrive, you'll know a bit about it. In fact, everything you have read in the book so far will be nothing like your own experience; I can guarantee that. BravoCon is so amazing, and next year, I tell myself I get to do it all over again with all new experiences!

For three full days, you will be living at the Forum. That's not going to change. Confirmed!

When you arrive at the Forum, there are many ways to get there, and walking is probably the best unless you're getting dropped off at the side entrance. The side entrance faces west, and the main drop-off is also the area where all the Bravolebs get dropped off, so if you get a few minutes, be sure to stop by there. The Forum has a roped off area so you can see the Bravolebs, and they do come over and say hi and take some fan pictures. If you get lucky, when you are getting dropped off or walking from the LINQ via the crosswalk, you might cross paths with some. I saw Sutton right as I was coming down the sidewalk. It was a BravoCon miracle! I got a picture and had to keep going. BravoCon is a fast-paced event, and she was off to have a day of fun. That's how it will be for you: if you randomly walk by a Bravoleb, you get a quick picture for a minute and then keep it going.

After you follow the sidewalk to the front of the Forum, you will see the huge platform entrance. You should enjoy this for a few minutes, walk around, and see everything happening. It almost appears like a small carnival is going on. Once you're done scoping everything, then you will see the roped off area to get in the Forum. Will call is also on the east side of the platform (I think). These folks can help you with lost tickets, picking up tickets, etc.

Once you are past security, you will see some fun Bravo signage. Be sure to take pictures, and then get your butt inside and enjoy the day!

Tips About the Forum

The Forum is huge and can be confusing when you are walking around, but take some time to do a quick tour so you know where the rooms you need to go. Walk the hallways, see the signage, and find out where the outside doors are to get to the back area for the rest area and photo ops. It's important you know so you can navigate quickly. Time flies between all these events!

Bathrooms

There is one main bathroom as soon as you walk in. Consider this your main bathroom. It has plenty of stalls and handicap stalls. If I recall correctly, it also has a baby changing station. I don't recall any babies at BravoCon, though. I think there are other bathrooms, but I don't really remember. I only went to that one, and it was very nice. I don't remember there being any lines, either.

Outside Back Patio (to get to the photo ops)

When you head out to the photo ops, you will most likely walk outside the Forum and be at the outside back patio to walk down the steps to the test. For me, the outside patio was the place to hang out, get some drinks, have a smoke and enjoy being outside! I loved going outside to take some well-needed breaks. There were no tables but long benches you could sit on. I thought it was very refreshing to have a place to just take a breath!

Disabled Access

I went as a disabled person with a mobility scooter and had no issues getting around, and the Forum was fantastic with the security to keep an eye on us. Offering extra help when needed, making sure we got in and out of places easier. It was wonderful.

Security

Most of us took pictures of our favorite security people. They become friends eventually if you see them enough. You can tell they enjoyed working at that event. I didn't have a negative experience with any of the security staff.

Panel Seating

These rooms have plenty of room, and the rush of getting to a panel day didn't happen in 2023. From what I saw, everything seems very managed, and I don't recall hearing any complaints about the lines. The rooms are so large; it's like a small auditorium but more intimate.

Hallways

It is very large and so wide that any Bravoleb can be seen coming right at you. Even if they have security all around them, you can still be on the side just fine. Yep, that happened to me many times. I loved how big this place was!

Backstage

There is no access to seeing the backstage areas. The black curtains are everywhere (black curtains mean you should not go behind them (unless invited). Once, I drove my scooter into an area where there was no security guard (I swear I thought I was finding a new room to explore) and saw a few Bravolebs standing around talking to each other. Frankly, I felt awkward, said hi, and then scooted myself out of there. I try to respect their private time. I try to remember that they are on stage all day, going here and there, and some of their time is for them, not us.

Parking

I didn't drive, nor do I know anyone who drove. So, unfortunately, I can't discuss parking.

Shopping

The Forum didn't have any stores or anything inside to buy. The food was in the Bravo Bazaar, and the bars were also in one place usually the whole time. It's not a venue that has shops and stores. Prepare to bring what you need for the event.

Food

The Bravo Bites are in the Bravo Bazaar, and they have food for sale there. There are no vending machines or anything, so if you're a foodie, this is not that type of event. However, you can get some tasty delights in the VIP lounge and Bravopalooza for a treat.

I could probably go on and on about the Forum; it was a great venue, and I look forward to so much.

CHAPTER 18

BRAVOLEBS AT BRAVOCON

They are everywhere at BravoCon! I know for most of you, meeting Bravolebs is your number one goal, and I know because it is all we talk about in the group. Pictures, meetings, stories, watching panels, getting a chance to talk to your favorites—that's what BravoCon is all about.

After you get the announcement of the Bravoleb's attendance, make that list and get working on your personal agenda. But what about the random sightings at BravoCon? There are plenty of ways to meet them in the wild or just at BravoCon unexpectedly. I consider this one of the best parts of BravoCon.

The first day you arrive in Vegas, just learn to keep your eyes peeled for them to pop up anytime, anywhere, and, of course, when you are not expecting to see one. You do not need to go crazy looking; they will just appear. The more you wander around the event, the more you will see them wandering around alone, with others, or with their security. Of course, the ones with security (Andrea from Summer House, Craig, and Andy Cohen were the three I noticed) are not "in the wild" as much at the Forum but maybe outside of the Forum.

At the event itself, the Bravolebs are scheduled to be at their events, so you know they will be there, close by, coming in or leaving. Some of the panels go off the stage and into the back, where we do not get to go, but for the Bravopaloozas, they come in and go out of the same doors we use. So, when you are waiting to get in one, the doors will open, and the Bravolebs will come out eventually, and you can see them. You might not get to talk to them, but you will see them.

Bravo Bazaar

By far the most popular place to see the Bravolebs in the wild. They might be at their merch booth or just wandering around.

Photo Ops

They will most likely be in their scheduled photo ops and not wandering around, but you can always check out the sides or back area that is open to the public. You might see one just hanging out. I am not saying that they want to be bothered, but that is up to you. I always feel a bit uncomfortable when I am prodding when I should not.

Hallways

The hallways are wonderful places to see Bravolebs. In the Forum, when you go to the right side of the Bravo Bazaar, there are huge hallways for everything on that side. If you have free time, wander around over there. You might see some come in and out of the rooms or the black curtains. I would not recommend hanging out there as it's mostly regular people like us coming and going, and we all are going fast! But hey, it is still a place to see them in the wild!

Bravopalooza

Some of these will have many Bravolebs scheduled for the photo op stage, and some will be there to "hang out" and not be in a photo op. It's kinda fun not to know who will be in the room with you and who actually wants to chat it up a bit. Keep your eyes open, as you might not recognize one standing right next to you!

Outside the Forum Entrance Area

The drop-off door entrance for the Bravolebs is not a secret by any means, but you can spot them getting out of their limos in the morning. There is a section roped off for you to stand a bit back and take pics. The Bravolebs sometimes come over for pictures and say hi or make short videos. I really enjoy this area; it is right across from the walkway of the LINQ hotel where I stay. If you are walking across the walkway, there is not much time to sit and watch. Security will scoot you by and ask you to keep moving or go behind the rope. Still, though, if you get there at the right time, you can see a Bravoleb coming out of a Limo all dressed up—a fun sight!

Meeting Bravolebs Tips

Last year, someone in the group mentioned that when you are up to meet a Bravoleb, keep your time respectable when others are waiting. The same goes for when you run into one not at a scheduled event or in the wild. It is always shocking to see one in the wild, and sometimes, they are shocked that they are being recognized. Remember, not every person in the world knows who a Bravoleb is, so when they are doing their day-to-day life, regular people do not stop and ask them for a photo. I always get a giggle when I think of all the Bravolebs in the airports getting noticed and the other travelers wondering what the heck is going on. Who is that person?

The Bravolebs will be everywhere you go, from your own airport to possibly being on your flight (it's quite common to hear this in the group) to staying at your hotel, dining where you are, walking by you—it's nuts!

If you follow them on Instagram, many of them document their trip to Vegas just like we do.

What Other "Bravolebs" Will Be There?

Many cast members from past shows who are not on a current Bravo TV show will also make appearances, so expect them to be there, too. You will also find a lot of other Bravoverse content creators there. They are taking pictures and videos and creating stories for their Instagram/TikTok channels. And randomly, you might run into other non-Bravolebs just roaming the hallways of BravoCon.

Gifts for the Bravolebs

I met people last year who brought a small gift for their favorite Bravoleb, like a friendship bracelet, and the Bravoleb put it on and wore it! If you want to do this, I would keep it very small. I did not see any Bravolebs with phones or purses or anything. They are on "stage" for the most part and can't take much with them. But it is a cute idea. I had people make me a friendship bracelet, and I have a stack I brought home. Super cute and thoughtful!

Where do They Hang Out?

At BravoCon, behind the black curtains. After they leave the Forum, they hang out in Vegas like we all do! Many people will post pictures of them spotting Bravolebs out and about. And they stay at the same hotels we will be at; they do tend to stay at a few of the same hotels, though. Each BravoCon, we tried to figure it out, but Vegas was different. Most Bravelebs did not just stay at one hotel but at many hotels. Personally, I am too busy to find them at hotels. I'm pretty tired after each day!

Other Bravoleb Events

If you have a favorite that is hosting their own event, sometimes other Bravolebs will attend as they are fans, too. You just never know in Vegas what will happen.

Best Experiences

My best experiences talking to Bravolebs were when they had more time in their photo ops to talk. Shane Simpson was my #1 as he was on the side of the stage watching Emily do her photo ops. JT from Southern Charm was my #2; we had an enjoyable time at the photo ops in the VIP lounge. I think I got in at the tail end of a line, and he had time to kill. This might be a good tip for you. Those lines are long to meet Bravolebs in the VIP lounge. Going last might be in your favor!

I met so many, though, and I enjoyed meeting them all. Sometimes, I was bummed I did not get enough time with some of my favorites, but that's how it goes at BravoCon. If you get your picture, treasure it. The conversations are always short for anyone at the event. I do think that many people had their own "fun story," though. You'll get yours!

CHAPTER 19

FINAL TIPS

A h, the final chapter! Just like day three of BravoCon, everything great has to end but will always live on forever on the internet. No one attends BravoCon without lifelong stories and memories. We will all share an experience that will be talked about for years. We will share pictures, videos, and memories with our online friends, in-person family and friends. We will create TikTok, Facebook Reels, Instagram posts and reels and discuss on Threads. For us, Bravoholics, Bravo TV and BravoCon are pure obsessions.

I hope you took everything that I wrote in the past 18 chapters and use what you need to help you. I also hope you enjoyed my stories and learning bit by bit everything I learned. For those of you who have gone to every BravoCon looking for that one tip that helps you, I hope you found it! For the new people coming, this entire book was created just for you! How to navigate the most amazing three days of your life! The rest of this chapter is just some odds and ends that you might want to know about or need later. And, of course, there will always be more to add. Bravo is the ultimate interactive experience! TV, social media, events, real-time drama, gossip—it's reality TV perfection.

Recap

From the past three BravoCons, there is a timeline for everything, and I covered it all from my own memory (all three events have had some changes, so be prepared. This list might change).

This will help new people to keep track of what to buy/expect and when or what to prepare. (The order might change). The entire BravoCon process, from announcements to the event, can be up to eight months long, but everything gets ramped up about 5 months before.

- Tickets announced
- Tickets go on sale
- WWHL goes on sale
- Photo Ops announced
- The app is updated
- Schedule is released
- The Panels
- BravoCon Live Stage
- After Dark goes on sale

After you're done reading this book, here are a few more important takeaways:

- I recommend reviewing the chapters about tickets once tickets are announced.

- Check the Patreon page for the "community chat" area of your tier (this is where everyone in the group can chat together in a private area, I can answer questions, etc.) I will have this created after the ticket sale date is announced.

- If you miss securing tickets after they are announced, then check back to the Patreon here and message me if you want to get on the waitlist. I will have the list in a Google Doc (using your initials and a number) open for everyone to see where they are in line. Remember, I'll be using the waitlist to help Facebook users sell tickets later on. There will be no more "open selling" in our group due to scammers and such.

The Patreon Site

Once you finish this book, be sure to subscribe to my Patreon page. Everyone can have a free membership. If you've never been a part of a Bravo "community," you are in for a treat! There, you will get all my live updates via email and won't miss any announcements, changes, or fun stuff I share. I also will have some merch available at some point you can purchase if you like.

https://www.patreon.com/UnofficialGuidetoBravoCon

BravoCon FAQ

As we get rolling, I will have some information posted here that was not in the book. Most posts will be new information, changes, updates, etc.

Here is the pinned post for the FAQ: https://www.patreon.com/posts/bravocon-faq-111447811

Other Questions

You will have your own questions, no doubt! I and the Facebook members will answer some questions; other questions, you might need to ask Bravo TV. They will have a customer service email at some point. They are sometimes busy during the event season, so it might be a bit for them to get back to you. Keep in mind that Bravo TV does not help with ticket sales, which is usually done through another company, but the ones in the past have had great customer service so far.

Ways to Ask Questions

- Post in the BravoCon Facebook Group
- Join our community chat on my Patreon page. I'll answer as many questions as I can. Others in the chat will most likely help, too. Everyone going to BravoCon is always helpful! https://www.patreon.com/UnofficialGuidetoBravoCon
- FAQ page. Once tickets go on sale, I will have a pinned FAQ page for BravoCon on my Patreon. I will update it with questions that weren't covered in my book or new questions that pop up.

Some Extra Tips!

Plan your trip home wisely. I cannot stress enough how much BravoCon can exhaust you. If you can take an extra day off work, I highly recommend that. I was so tired when I got home that all I wanted to do was rest. Give your little legs a break, put them up, and enjoy not doing anything!

Sharing Pictures after BravoCon

Many people will share their pictures in the BravoCon Facebook Group in real time as they arrive in Vegas until they get home. Some like to organize and post on their own socials and then in our group. The group is so wild during our event; we will have over 200,000 videos, pictures, comments, and reactions. It's our busy season, and sometimes, sharing the pictures later is a good idea, especially if you want to tell a story about the pictures. If you want to wait a week, no worries—people will be posting for a month or so. The group usually calms down about a month later, then we go back to discussing our favorite topic, Bravo TV and Bravolebs!

Here are my social media accounts if you want to follow:
- **My Instagram account:**
  https://www.instagram.com/queenofbravocon
- **My Facebook:**
  https://www.Facebook.com/lisa.hendrickson
- **My TikTok:**

https://www.tiktok.com/@queenofbravocon

- **My Facebook Page:**

  https://www.Facebook.com/queenofbravocon

THANK YOU TIME!

Thank you for buying this book! I'm sure you are so excited to enjoy every single minute and moment that BravoCon gives. I know you have your own great stories and forever memories to share.

The B's of the BravoCon Facebook Group! Thank you all!!!! The BravoCon Facebook Group is literally my sisterhood that I never thought I'd ever have or need. It is seriously my daily joy, and I love chatting with so many members. Even though we have a long wait until the next BravoCon, it will come before we know it, and we will get to see each other again!

A huge thank you to Suzy McGonigle for joining me on this 5-year anniversary of BravoCon! She and I have been each other's support system, and I am so glad I have a Bravo Bestie to text with, laugh with, and enjoy so many memories at BravoCon with.

The mod team! Angi, Sharri, Jamie, and Kim—all of these women support the BravoCon Facebook Group, helping it stay nice and cool; they kick out all the uncool people! We learn each BravoCon how it works and work together as a mod squad. Everyone is unpaid and does it for the love of Bravo!

Special shout out to Lindsey Clark for helping me get through my first draft of this book. Her feedback was super valuable. She also helped with the Google Docs schedule.

The Bravo TV staff! Ellen Stone, Jennifer Geisser, and the social media team. Without your support, the BravoCon Facebook Group would not be what it is today! We love that you support small communities of Bravo TV fans and show it even in our off-season! Bravo TV always keeps their fans in mind whatever they do, and it shows their commitment to staying in touch with all of us.

Finally, thank you to my best friend Mary, who has always encouraged me to write, tell my stories, and lift me up when I'm feeling down. Mary doesn't watch Bravo, but she knows plenty about it from all my years of being in the Bravo Sphere!

Can't wait to see everyone in Vegas. Until then, signing off!

Queen of the B's!

Lisa, love ya!! XOXO

ABOUT THE AUTHOR

Lisa Hendrickson has been captivated by reality TV since the early 2000s, with her first Bravo obsession being *Queer Eye for the Straight Guy*. Since then, her love for all things Bravo has only deepened. Residing in Minnesota, Lisa balances her career as an independent Microsoft Expert with her passion for the Bravoverse. She manages a thriving BravoCon Facebook community, stays plugged into the latest online drama, and channels her insights into engaging videos and her book, *72 Hours of Unfiltered: 72 Hours Unscripted: How to Navigate the Ultimate 3-Day Bravoleb Weekend.*

Made in the USA
Columbia, SC
12 May 2025

57853605R00076